ADSCAM

How Online Advertising Gave Birth to One of History's
Greatest Frauds, and Became a Threat to Democracy

BOB HOFFMAN

TYPE A

Type A Group, Oakland

ADSCAM by Bob Hoffman

Cover Design: Bob Hoffman/Bonnie Miguel

Interior Design: Bonnie Miguel

Publisher: Type A Group, LLC

For information contact: bob@typeagroup.com

ISBN 978-0-9992307-4-9

Also by Bob Hoffman

101 Contrarian Ideas About Advertising

Marketers Are From Mars, Consumers Are From New Jersey

BadMen: How Advertising Went From A Minor Annoyance To A Major Menace

Laughing@Advertising

Advertising For Skeptics

About the Author

Bob Hoffman is a writer and speaker. He is the author of five Amazon number one selling books about advertising.

Bob has been the chief executive of two independent ad agencies and the U.S. operation of an international agency.

He is one of the most sought-after international speakers on advertising and marketing. He has been invited to speak in twenty-four countries. In 2021 he was invited to speak to members of the British Parliament. In 2022 he was asked to speak to the European Commission.

Bob's blog and newsletter, *The Ad Contrarian*, was named one of the world's most influential marketing and advertising blogs by Business Insider. His commentary has appeared in the BBC World Service, The Wall Street Journal, The New York Times, MSNBC, The Financial Times, The Australian, New Zealand Public Broadcasting, Fox News, Sky News, Forbes, Canadian Public Broadcasting, and many other news outlets throughout the world.

One of his books, *BadMen: How Advertising Went From A Minor Annoyance To A Major Menace*, exposed many of the dangerous privacy abuse practices that have gone on to make international headlines. It was selected "Best of Marketing 2017".

In 2012 Bob was selected "Ad Person of the Year" by the San Francisco Advertising Club.

He has served on the boards of the Advertising and Marketing International Network, the Foundation for Osteoporosis Research and Education, and the PGA Foundation of Northern California. He spent one year as Special Assistant to the Executive Director of the California Academy of Sciences.

Praise for Bob

"FABULOUSLY IRREVERENT" – *Time, Inc*

"IF YOU DON'T KNOW WHO BOB HOFFMAN IS THEN YOU
REALLY DON'T WORK IN ADVERTISING. THAT, OR YOU HAVE
NOT STEEPED YOURSELF IN THE WISDOM OF THIS MAN."
– *MediaPost*

"CAUSTIC YET TRUTHFUL" – *The Wall Street Journal*

"THE MOST PROVOCATIVE MAN IN ADVERTISING" – *Fuel Lines*

"SAVAGE CRITIQUES OF DIGITAL HYPE" – *Financial Times*

"IT'S NICE TO FIND A REAL THINKER IN THE AD BUSINESS
THESE DAYS" – *Jack Trout, Forbes*

"BOB IS THE LITTLE CHILD WHO POINTS OUT THAT
THE EMPEROR IS WEARING NO CLOTHES … I'M JEALOUS.
I WISH I'D BEEN BRAVE ENOUGH TO BE THIS RUDE."
– *Prof. Byron Sharp, author, "How Brands Grow"*

"ONE OF OUR TRULY GREAT MARKETING ICONOCLASTS"
– *Mark Ritson*

"BOB HOFFMAN…IS POSSIBLY GOING TO BE SEEN AS THE
MOST INFLUENTIAL PERSON OF THE DECADE WHEN IT
COMES TO MEDIA"   – *Tom Denford, CEO, ID Comms*

Dedication

For Marmy, Billy, and Joanney

Introduction

The first thing that appeared in my 2017 book, *BadMen,* was a reference to a then unknown company named *Cambridge Analytica.* Within eight months it became one of the most famous companies in the world.

While many in the advertising and marketing industry knew full well the dangerous game of surveillance and exploitation that was being played by online advertisers, front page headlines about Cambridge Analytica all across the globe brought the dangers of tracking-based media to the attention of hundreds of millions for the first time.

Since the exposure of Cambridge Analytica, privacy abuse by the adtech industry has become a cause célèbre among chattering politicians and regulators. Sadly, their posturing and bloviating has had little to no effect on the ability of the huge adtech platforms to follow us everywhere and intrude on all aspects of our public and private activities.

It is now five years later and the damage done by online advertising is substantially greater than it was then. Specifically, this book adds facts and commentary about three very troubling aspects of online advertising that are not often discussed in polite company:

- How online advertising has contributed to the dangerous, destructive wedge that has developed in the political life of democratic nations.

- How online advertising has enabled the annual transfer of tens of billions of dollars from legitimate businesses to criminal enterprises and other potential malefactors through one of the largest frauds the world has ever known.

- How the leaders of the advertising and marketing industry have turned a blind eye to the damage that tracking-based marketing tactics have done to the public.

The mechanism that enables these outrages is the practice of spying on people across the web; relentlessly collecting private and personal information about people; sharing and selling that information to anyone who wants it. This has caused enormous, often unseen, damage to individuals and to society.

I have attempted to write a short, simple book that tells the story succinctly, without filler or flourishes. The book consists of some new pieces and some I have edited from previously published articles and essays. It is written mostly as a series of essays about a wide variety of topics touching on the technology known as "adtech." While each piece is just a slim slice, I hope that taken as a whole these slices will suggest the broad scope of the problem we are facing.

Democratic societies are experiencing unprecedented dangers as a result of deep divisions among the citizenry. Businesses are losing tens of billions of dollars annually to criminals. To varying degrees, these two problems have a common source—the practice of online tracking of individuals to collect and exploit personal, private information about us. This book tells a small part of that story.

Author's Notes

I have not been coy about my opinions. I believe tracking-based advertising has created serious perils for individuals and for democratic societies and I'm not timid about stating that opinion.

You will notice that among the stories I relate concerning malfeasance, lying, and cheating, I often single out Facebook. It's not that they are the only dangerous company in the adtech world, it's that I have a particular dislike for them. I'm not going to pretend that this dislike is in any way unbiased. In my opinion they are a despicable enterprise that has lied and cheated its way to success. And I'm not going to refer to them as "Meta." They can call themselves whatever the hell they like. As far as I'm concerned they'll never get the stink of Facebook off them, whatever they pretend to be.

I've tried to write this book in a fashion that will be useful to advertising professionals, but also comprehensible to civilians. I have been surprised by the large number of people in the advertising and marketing industry who know the *language* of adtech, but don't really understand the workings of adtech.

There is a lot going on under the hood of the online ad industry that is incomprehensible to people who are not computer scientists. In no way is this book an attempt to delve into the ones and zeroes. If I understood that stuff I'd be happy to explain it. But, for better or worse, I don't.

Instead, you'll be reading the thoughts of someone a lot like you who can't understand for the life of him how something as silly as advertising became so dangerous.

Alphabet Soup

A glossary of some of the annoying advertising acronyms, abbreviations and jargon that will be irritating you throughout this book.

4A's: (American Association of Advertising Agencies) Trade organization representing the advertising agencies in the U.S.

Adtech: The use of computer technology to buy, sell, and distribute advertising online.

Ad fraud: Activity by which advertising money is diverted from legitimate media to criminals.

ANA: (Association of National Advertisers) Trade organization representing virtually all the big advertisers in the U.S.

CCPA: (California Consumer Privacy Act) Legislation passed by the State of California to protect consumer privacy. Similar, but not identical to GDPR (see below.)

DSP: Demand-Side Platform. Software that helps automate the buying of advertising.

GDPR: (General Data Protection Regulation) Europe's comprehensive regulation designed to protect consumers from privacy abuse by the adtech industry.

IAB: (Interactive Advertising Bureau) The adtech industry's trade organization.

ISBA: (Incorporated Society of British Advertisers) The U.K.'s equivalent of the ANA.

Programmatic Advertising: Online advertising that is bought, sold, and distributed by computer systems instead of humans.

RTB: (Real-Time Bidding) The foundation on which the automated (programmatic) online advertising industry is built. Every time you go to a web page several auctions are held. The auctions decide who can show you ads on that web page. The auctions take place in nanoseconds. The winning bidders (this is all done by computers) get to have their ads displayed on the page you are viewing.

SSP: Supply-Side Platform. Software that helps automate the selling of advertising.

TCF: (Transparency & Consent Framework) A construct of the adtech industry which was developed to try to conform the practice of tracking to the legal restrictions on tracking. The primary manifestations of TCF are the pop-ups you get when you go to a website and they ask you to "allow all" tracking. The TCF has been ruled to be illegal in Europe.

WFA: The World Federation of Advertisers. A trade association representing the interests of most of the world's largest advertisers.

Okay, take a deep breath and let's move on.

Contents

Part One: Danger

What Is Adtech?

Everywhere we go on the web we are being followed. Everything we do on the web is being catalogued. This is called tracking. Tracking is just a pleasanter word for surveillance.

By tracking us, marketers know who we talk to, what we say, where we go, and what we do. They know who our friends are, what our interests are, what our bank balances look like, what our sexual preferences are, what our political leanings are, and where we are at any moment. They exploit this information in two ways: by using it to sell us stuff, and by reselling it to other marketers. The consequences of all this surveillance have become shocking, disturbing, and dangerous.

Tracking also powers what we in the ad industry call adtech. Adtech started simply and benignly as a computerized (automated) method for buying, selling, and distributing advertising online. It has morphed into a monster. It has been reported that by the time an average child is thirteen years old, the adtech industry has 72,000,000 data points on that child.

To understand adtech we have to understand that online advertising is different from other forms of advertising in one very important way. In traditional advertising an advertiser buys advertising space from a publisher, like *The New York Times*. You buy a page in *The Times* for next Sunday, and you can see your ad right there in the newspaper next Sunday.

In most cases, online advertising is bought differently. Advertisers don't buy an ad unit, they buy *a type of person*. What adtech does is track each of us around the web and delivers ads to us anywhere we go. So when companies are buying "programmatic" (automated) online advertising, they are usually not buying space directly from a website publisher, and they often have no idea where on the web their ad may land. Instead they ask the online ad system to find a person like you and deliver ads to you wherever you may be online.

The purported benefit to the advertiser is this. Instead of reaching Bob Hoffman by running their ad on *The New York Times* website, where it might cost $1 to reach Bob, they can track Bob to *bikinibeachbabes(dot)com*, a much lower quality website, where they can run the same ad and it may cost them only a nickel. The only problem is that *bikinibeachbabes(dot)com* may not be a real website, and Bob Hoffman may not be a real person. We'll get to that soon.

In a study of some of the U.K.'s largest advertisers (including Disney, Shell, Lloyds, PepsiCo and Unilever) the Incorporated Society of British Advertisers (ISBA) found that ads bought programmatically for the average advertiser wound up on over 40,000 different websites, over 80% of which were "not premium". Not premium is a nice British way of saying crap.

As we will see, many of these "not premium" websites don't actually exist. Many others exist with imaginary audiences. And many "not smart" advertisers are spending enormous amounts of money on these "not premium" websites.

In the real world, the online advertising supply chain is so replete with garbage that displaying an ad on some websites costs tenths or even hundredths of a penny. On the surface, the value proposition of ad tech - reaching the highest quality eyeballs at the cheapest possible locations - is an appealing proposition. But as we shall see, advertising has probably never experienced a wider gap between promise and reality. This has led to all kinds of expensive and dangerous consequences.

It has enabled a cesspool of corruption and an ocean of fraud.

It places personal and private information about us easily within the reach of criminals, unfriendly governments, and other potential malefactors.

It has devalued the work of legitimate online publishers.

It has degraded news media and journalism.

It is distrusted by marketers and is despised by the public. According to recent research, advertising people are the world's least trusted.

It delivers the advertising of reputable companies to disreputable sites.

And, as we will see, it has played a major role in driving a perilous wedge into our culture.

Other than that, it's great.

Adtech and Sugar

To understand why adtech has been so totally and naively embraced by the advertising industry a simple history lesson is instructive.

For a good part of human history food didn't taste very good. That's why spices from the Far East were such treasured commodities in the West. In the seventeenth century sugar imported from New Guinea and India became more easily available in England and became very popular. One of the prime reasons was that it made tea taste a lot better. But the Brits went overboard. They couldn't get enough of the stuff. In 1700 the average Brit consumed about four pounds of sugar. By 1900 the annual per capita consumption was ninety pounds.

Until experience kicks in we never know what the effects of a newly acquired enthusiasm are going to be. At first, the English didn't know the effects sugar had on teeth. It is reported that Queen Elizabeth's teeth turned black from sugar. Not that long ago, many women in England had their teeth extracted in their twenties.

When something comes along that magically satisfies a perceived need or craving there can be harsh and unintended consequences. The release from deprivation can create an obsession for the source of relief. Ask any sailor.

In the 20th century the advertising industry had a gaping deficiency. We had very little scientifically reliable information on the efficacy of advertising. Mostly, we had anecdotes and case histories - in other words, bullshit tarted up to look like facts.

The 21st century brought us marketing technology. And with technology came the promise of science and an enormous appetite for data, measurement, and mathematics. These are important aspects of advertising when consumed in reasonable quantities. But when the craving for numbers becomes a mania, there are sure to be unintended consequences.

Ad people have been kicked around for a long time because our discipline has been devoid of the benefits of reliable science When seemingly relevant technology came along we went from four pounds to ninety pounds in about ten minutes. We are now swallowing all the technology we can stuff into our mouths as quickly as we can, regardless of its relevance, reliability, authenticity, or side effects.

Desperately hungry for the gratification of numbers, we are gorging on technology and finding that our frenzied indulgence is rotting our teeth. And, as we shall see, ironically, the metrics that adtech has produced for the ad industry are among the least reliable metrics we've ever had.

Targeted Advertising

You are more likely to sell golf balls to golfers than to chess players. So you run ads for golf balls in golf magazines, not chess magazines.

You are more likely to sell lipstick to women than you are to men. So you run ads for lipstick in media that cater to women.

You are more likely to sell Monster Energy drink to idiots than you are to brain surgeons. So you target teenagers.

There is nothing nefarious about any of this, it is just basic business sense. It is what we call "targeting". Targeting is based on the simple principle that you have a better chance of selling your stuff by directing your messages to people who are more likely to buy it.

Many critics of tracking-based advertising mistakenly call it "targeted advertising." This is wrong. All advertising is targeted. The difference between tracking-based advertising and traditional advertising is not that it is targeted, but how the targets are derived.

Before tracking, ad targets were developed mostly from non-personal public records like census information, TV and radio ratings, newspaper circulation numbers, and primary research commissioned by advertisers. We did not collect personal, private information about individuals.

The most important concept that needs to be understood about adtech is that the basic process that underlies its current model is tracking. Virtually everything that the adtech industry does originates with the data they collect from tracking each of us as we move about the web.

One of adtech's most compelling promises to the business community is that by tracking us, they can make the targeting of advertising far more precise. By making targeting more precise, they claim they can save advertisers money by also making it significantly more efficient. (I have argued strenuously against "precision targeting" as a source of advertising efficacy in other books - see *Advertising For Skeptics* - but let's leave that argument for another day.)

The difference between ad targeting based on non-personal data like demographics, and ad targeting based on personal data derived from tracking may seem academic on the surface. But as we shall see, the difference is stark and unnerving.

On the Dangers of Tracking

This piece is based on a presentation I gave to a group of Members of the British Parliament in July of 2021.

Advertising's traditional job has been to impart information to people. Today, however, certain types of advertising have become equally concerned with collecting information about people. Doc Searls, author of *The Intention Economy,* says that a good deal of online advertising can be viewed as spyware that only looks like advertising.

Most researchers estimate that about five online display ads out of 10,000 get clicked on. But almost every one of those 10,000 ads is capable of harvesting information about the person the ad is delivered to.

I'm not a computer scientist or a software engineer. Trying to understand the arcane technology of digital advertising is above my pay grade. But you don't have to be an automotive engineer to understand that a truck can run you over.

In 2017 I wrote *BadMen: How Advertising Went from a Minor Annoyance to a Major Menace.* In that book I wrote that we know the dangers that accrue when governments know everything about us, follow us everywhere, read our communications, and know who we talk to and what we talk about. We know this because history has shown us the horrors of governmental organs like the Stasi, the Gestapo, and the KGB. But we don't know what can occur when *marketers* know everything about us. When *they* follow us everywhere, read our communications, and know who we talk to and what we talk about.

I wrote that five years ago. Sadly, today we are starting to understand what those dangers are.

There is nothing ambiguous about the role the marketing and advertising industry has played in the radicalization of politics here in the United States and the horrifying, violent events in January 2021 in Washington D.C. There is a clear line connecting online tracking by advertisers and political radicalization and destabilization.

THE STRAIGHT LINE BETWEEN ADTECH AND RADICALIZATION

TRACKING ▶ **ALGORITHMS** ▶ **RABBIT HOLES** ▶ **RADICALIZATION**

Tracking collects data (information) about people and feeds it to algorithms.	Algorithms use the data to deliver more "engaging"- often more sensational - content.	Sensational content drives people to "rabbit holes" where the most extreme elements reside.	Radicalization leads to nothing but trouble.

As we move about the web, trackers relentlessly gather information about where we go, what we look at, and what we interact with. This information is then fed into algorithms which are formulas derived from our behavior and, to some extent, describe our personalities. The algorithms are used by platforms to decide what to show us. For example, my Facebook page is completely different from yours. It is based on the algorithms that describe me. My page shows me content that is likely to be more engaging to me. Your page shows you content that is likely to be more engaging to you.

The purpose of these algorithms is primarily to keep us "inside the corral" of the publisher or the platform. The more time I spend inside their corral, the more money the platform can realize from selling space on my page to advertisers. To do this, the platforms feed me ever more "engaging" content. Experience has taught the algorithms that the more juicy the material, the more likely they are to keep me inside the corral.

Consequently, the algorithms often feed me incrementally more lurid notions of my own predispositions. Driving me deeper into rabbit holes where I may encounter people whose ideas are more extreme versions of my own.

In May of 2020, *The Wall Street Journal* reported that after the U.S. presidential election of 2016, a team of Facebook executives undertook an internal study to understand how these practices shaped the behavior of its users. The study concluded that the algorithms they use to gain user attention and increase time on their platform were driving a wedge into U.S. society.

According to the report, *"64% of all extremist group joins are due to our recommendation tools ... Our recommendation systems grow the problem."*

This report revealed the truth. It unambiguously described the way social algorithms direct people into extremist groups of all kinds. And it's all driven by tracking.

Professor Hany Farid, an expert at University of California, Berkeley, has said, *"They didn't set out to fuel misinformation and hate and divisiveness, but that's what the algorithms learned."*

Facebook would like us to believe that it is simply a bulletin board where people are free to post their beliefs and that this is healthy for society. The *Wall Street Journal* report revealed the truth. It described the way these platforms direct people into extremist groups of all stripes. Surveillance marketing is little more than ten years' old but it has already helped drive a wedge of intolerance into democratic societies.

The effect on U.S. society has been stunning. The graph below shows how dangerously polarized the American electorate has become in just twenty years.

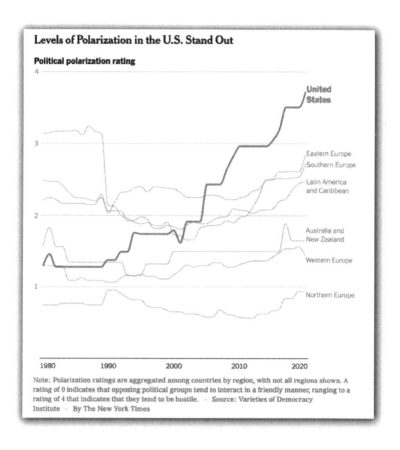

Levels of Polarization in the U.S. Stand Out

Political polarization rating

Note: Polarization ratings are aggregated among countries by region, with not all regions shown. A rating of 0 indicates that opposing political groups tend to interact in a friendly manner, ranging to a rating of 4 that indicates that they tend to be hostile.   ·   Source: Varieties of Democracy Institute   ·   By The New York Times

But there's more to this story. For years, the ad industry has been hiding behind the skirts of Facebook and other online platforms. While these companies have taken the heat, it has been largely unrecognized by the public that this squalid work has been carried out for the sole benefit of the advertising and marketing industry. We are the hidden hand that guides and finances these dangerous practices.

And how does the advertising industry justify the damage we are doing?

It is through a series of disingenuous assertions about the supposed benefits of surveillance. The first and most dishonest of the claims is that the free internet is reliant on surveillance for its revenue model. This is simply not true. Traditional media—TV, radio, press, outdoor—did very well for decades without tracking. There is no reason online advertising can't be viable without spying on us. Over many decades, the advertising industry has proven itself to be brilliant at finding appropriate buyers for products. We have done it mostly with "light touch" targeting that does not abuse the privacy of individuals.

The internet has many things that we all love. And, yes, advertising funds this free stuff. But tracking and surveillance do not. Is the free internet reliant on advertising? Yes. Is it reliant on tracking? No.

Next we hear that tracking is necessary because consumers want more relevant advertising. Nonsense! In 2021 Apple changed its operating system to give its iPhone and iPad users the choice of being tracked or not. Eighty percent of people in the U.S. chose not to be tracked.

Let's play devil's advocate for a moment and pretend that the marketers' need for spying on the public is essential to their business model. The question I would pose is this: *Since when did the convenience of marketers become more important than the privacy rights of individuals and the integrity of democratic institutions?*

Online advertising supports many good things that we enjoy and appreciate about the web. It gives us free entertainment and free information. It allows us to befriend people we would otherwise never meet. It would take so little for the digital ad industry to do so much good for itself and for the public.

Ending tracking, ending surveillance, ending spying on the public is not a panacea for all the problems of the digital world, but it is a great place to start. We need to get rid of tracking—not advertising—to help make the web be what it ought to be.

Ad Targeting by Algorithm

To give a specific example of how algorithms used by platforms like Facebook drive people apart, here's a wonderful illustration from *The Markup* via NYU's *Cybersecurity for Democracy* project.

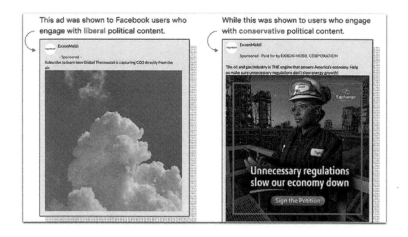

In this example we see two different ads from the same company— ExxonMobil—that appeared on Facebook. The first ad was targeted at people who the Facebook algorithm determined were liberals. It spoke of ExxonMobil's commitment to environmental concerns. The second ad was targeted at people whom the Facebook algorithm determined were conservative, and spoke of the *problem* of environmental regulations.

Tracking us and maintaining surveillance over our every move informs the algorithms that divide us into warring camps and elevates the probability that we only see content that reinforces our biases. What may be even worse is that we often do not know the identity of the organizations behind the ads served on our Facebook page. Work by NYU's *Cybersecurity for Democracy* project reported that during a 13-month period ending in June of 2019, the identity of the sponsors of political ads running on Facebook had been concealed more than half the time. This violated Facebook's own rules.

What did Facebook do as a result? They suspended the accounts of the academics doing the research. The head of the research group at NYU had this to say, *"We cannot be beholden to Facebook for which pieces of research we do and don't do. If we do that, we're not independent researchers. What happened to us isn't just about us. Facebook is sending a warning to other researchers. If Facebook doesn't like your research, if they don't like how you do it or what your findings are, they're going to find a way to retaliate against you."*

Civil War by Algorithm

You're probably going to think I'm being hysterical, and I hope you're right. I would love to stop writing about politics and get back to writing about advertising. Unfortunately, there is now a toxic connection between the two that cannot be ignored.

Let's review some history. In the entirety of what we laughingly call "civilization" there has never been a government that has survived. Not one. Not ever. Sooner or later they all get overthrown and replaced. What reason do we have to believe that democratic governments are exempt from history? Correct, none.

Social media is largely tens of millions of unpleasant people looking to make trouble. A company called, *Arkose Labs*, did a real-time study of over 1 billion social media interactions. They found that 53% of the logins were fraudulent. Many social media scammers are just in it for the money. But some of the most successful social media troublemakers have been exploiters of lies, misinformation and political alienation.

When the history of this era is written, one of the key themes will be the remarkable success that social media manipulators had on influencing and exacerbating the divisions in democratic societies. They didn't invent the divisions, but they have become brilliantly adept at exploiting and inflaming them. Here in the U.S. there was a time when intelligent people of good will could disagree in a civilized manner. Those days are gone.

We may be in the first stages of what could turn out to be a death spiral for our form of government. To a significant degree, this horrifying possibility is being driven by the advertising and marketing industry.

You don't have to be a sociologist to recognize that a substantial amount of the radical polarization in this country has been propelled by ultra-factionalization on social media. The growing wedge that has appeared in our culture and our society has been driven significantly by the hidden hand of digital algorithms.

The oxygen that makes these algorithms effective and noxious is the information about us that is collected through online tracking by advertisers, marketers, and their surrogates in the media. The relentless collection of online data that feeds the toxic algorithms tearing our society apart is being effectuated on behalf of the advertising and marketing industry. The so-called leadership of our industry—the trade organizations, the CEOs of agencies and holding companies, the C-somethings of brands and media—have not been tacit bystanders to all this. They have been active cheerleaders for the continued collection of information that powers the algorithms and inflames the divisions. For over ten years, they have opposed every serious regulatory initiative to limit personal data collection and exploitation.

The question is, have we learned anything? Do we have the wisdom to do a mid-course correction? If not, we are now headed for ten years that will be infinitely worse.

Profiting from Hate

On July 1, 2021, Facebook's VP of global affairs and communications, Nick Clegg, stated, *"I want to be unambiguous: Facebook does not profit from hate."*

I would also like to be unambiguous: *Bullshit!*

Facebook makes over 98% of its money from advertising. The way you make money from advertising is by attracting people to your site. This is the same for other media like TV, radio, and newspapers. The more people you attract, and the longer they stay, the more money you can extract from advertisers.

As discussed in a previous chapter, when you go to Facebook you are shown a completely different page than I see when I go to Facebook. Your page has your friends, ads from companies that Facebook thinks you will be interested in, and posts that Facebook thinks you will like. Mine has completely different friends, different ads, and different posts. The decisions about what to show each of us are made in milliseconds by algorithms. The algorithms constantly evolve in ways that are aimed at maintaining our interest. This is how we are encouraged to keep coming back to Facebook and staying as long as possible.

You may be surprised to know that the data Facebook gathers about you is not simply from your behaviors on Facebook, but on all kinds of other behaviors even if you are not a Facebook user, and even if you have opted out of tracking. At one point I calculated that Facebook's terms of service and privacy policies are longer than the U.S. Constitution. Here are some of the things their privacy policies allow them to do:

- Facebook maintains the right to collect your phone number and other information about you when anyone, including people you don't know, upload their contacts that may include you.
- Even when you *turn off* location services, Facebook tracks your location through Wi-Fi access points, cell towers and IP addresses.
- You probably think Facebook is collecting data about you from the device you're using. Silly you. If you are *anywhere near any other devices* on your network they are collecting info from those devices as well. It's magic!
- Facebook tracks you through third parties *whether or not* you are logged into Facebook.
- And the pièce de résistance—Facebook's data policy asserts that they track you *even if you don't have a Facebook account.*

Now, back to "not profiting from hate," the online media industry has learned that one of the most powerful tools to keep people engaged is controversy. Many studies have shown that hate speech is powerful stuff. According to one study, *"...content generated by the hateful users tend to spread faster, farther and reach a much wider audience as compared to the content generated by normal users."*

This is not a pleasant fact, but it is a fact nonetheless.

A comprehensive study by NYU and the Université Grenoble Alpes in France has found that, *"Misinformation on Facebook got six times more clicks than factual news during the 2020 election."* The researchers found that between August 2020 and January 2021, posts from publishers known to traffic in misinformation got six times as many likes, shares, and interactions as posts from reliable organizations.

In defense, a Facebook spokesquid said, *"This report looks mostly at how people engage with content, which should not be confused with how many people actually see it on Facebook ... "*

Oh.

Algorithms learned about the power of misinformation very early on and have been designed to serve us emotionally powerful material that will keep us engaged. At times, this material can be divisive and hateful and feed into the most negative aspects of our personalities. For the most part, algorithms don't make value judgements. They simply feed us material that will keep us in the corral for as long as possible.

Facebook goes beyond that. As mentioned in the previous section, Facebook actively seeks to keep us further engaged by recommending "groups" to us that its algorithms believe we will find attractive. These may be perfectly innocent groups about fashion, baseball, or books. Or they may be thinly disguised groups of pedophiles, criminals, and advocates of hate and violence. Facebook's algorithms help extremists of all kinds find each other, engage with each other, stay longer on the platform, and therefore create the opportunity for Facebook to earn more ad dollars.

It may be true that Facebook didn't set out to "profit from hate" but for years Facebook has been unambiguously directing their users to hateful groups. Why? Because it is profitable.

In order to believe Mr. Clegg's claim that Facebook does not profit from hate, you have to believe that Mark Zuckerberg doesn't understand how his algorithms work. And if you believe that, I'm afraid you will believe anything.

My favorite Mark Zuckerberg quote: *"I've developed a deep appreciation for how building a strong company with a strong economic engine and strong growth can be the best way to align many people to solve important problems."*

I can't help but wonder what important problems Mr. Zuckerberg thinks he has solved.

Bad for the World. Good for Us.

There is a robust catalog of studies, commentary and case histories regarding how social media, and the algorithms it employs have negatively affected social relations. My intention is not to review all these cases, but I would like to focus on one

A slide from the Facebook presentation described in a previous section said, *"Our algorithms exploit the human brain's attraction to divisiveness."* If left unchecked, it warned, Facebook would feed users. *"...more and more divisive content in an effort to gain user attention and increase time on the platform."*

This was prophetic.

Eight months before the January 6, 2021 riot at the Capitol in Washington D.C., the *Wall Street Journal* ran a story reporting that, *"Facebook is under fire for making the world more divided. Many of its own experts appeared to agree... and to believe Facebook could mitigate many of the problems. The company chose not to."*

According to *The New York Times*, soon after the 2020 election, *"...a team of Facebook employees presented the chief executive, Mark Zuckerberg, with an alarming finding: Election-related misinformation was going viral on the site."*

It is common knowledge in social media circles that posts that are false, sensational, slanderous, and scurrilous are far more engaging than posts that are faithful to the truth. According to a study by MIT, tweets that carry false news travel six times faster on Twitter and are 70% more likely to be retweeted than truthful tweets. Facebook executives refer to these type of false posts as "bad-for-the-world" posts. Soon after the 2020 election, posts deemed "bad-for-the-world" by Facebook executives were going viral.

In response to this situation, Facebook ran an experiment in which they changed their algorithm to de-emphasize the "bad-for-the-world" posts. According to *The Times*, *"In early tests, the new algorithm successfully reduced the visibility of objectionable content. But it also lowered the number of times users opened Facebook..."*

In other words, Facebook had a choice to make. They could reduce the number of posts they deemed "bad-for-the-world," but this might not be good-for-business. Did Facebook implement this good-for-the-world change in its algorithm?

You're kidding, right?

Side Effects Are the Important Effects

The polarizing effect of tracking-based algorithms used by platforms is largely not understood, even by very smart people. A piece in *The New York Times* entitled *"America Has Split, and It's Now in 'Very Dangerous Territory'"* describes how polarization is ripping society apart.

After more than 10 years of writing about the scourge of tracking and online surveillance, it finally occurred to me recently why most people, regulators, and legislators don't seem to get it or care much about it. I was at a dinner with a famous economist, and a former professor of marketing at one of our most prestigious universities. Over the course of dinner the topic of conversation turned to online advertising.

I explained how I felt about tracking-based online advertising. One of these brilliant people replied, *"I don't see what all the fuss is about. Sure, online advertising sometimes feels creepy. But so what? All advertising is creepy."*

At that moment the penny dropped. I realized for the first time what the problem is. The worst consequences of tracking are not that it makes *advertising* worse, it's that it makes *other things* so dangerous. What most people don't understand is that the tracking-based data collected by and for advertisers is also used:

- To create algorithms that have the effect of polarizing us and driving wedges into society.
- By malefactors to spread misinformation and lies in specific directions undermining confidence in elections, democratic institutions and scientific findings.
- By criminals to extract tens of billions of dollars illegally from the programmatic advertising ecosystem.

Like so many advertising and marketing people, I made the mistake of forgetting that advertising is of little consequence to most people. They really don't give a flying shit about it and if it's a little more annoying, so what? In order for us to get people to understand the damage that tracking is doing, we need to change the context of the argument away from advertising itself and explain what the reckless practice of tracking is doing outside its effect on ads.

Which leads us here…

"I Have Nothing to Hide"

In 2010, I wrote my first piece about the ad industry's assault on privacy. It appeared in *Adweek* magazine and was called, *"Big Brother Has Arrived, And He's Us."* Since then, I have written and spoken almost weekly about the dangers to individuals and to society from tracking and adtech.

Most of the time my musings were shrugged off with a simple, *"I don't worry about tracking. I have nothing to hide."* I heard this response most frequently from young people. As is often the case, "young people" was just a euphemism for "stupid people."

The Supreme Court decision overturning Roe v Wade has brought to light the very concrete and very real jeopardy that adtech and tracking create for individuals, in particular women:

- A report by *Reveal* and *The Markup* found that *"Facebook is collecting ultra-sensitive personal data about abortion seekers and enabling anti-abortion organizations to use that data as a tool to target and influence people online ..."*
- According to *The Markup*, 33 of the nation's top 100 hospitals have a Facebook "pixel" (a tracking device) on their websites that sends Facebook the IP address of anyone who goes to one of these sites.
- According to *MSN*, *"...the intricate web of data collected by fertility apps, tech companies and data brokers might be used (by police) to prove a violation of abortion restrictions ..."*
- The *Washington Post* says, *"Google's unprecedented hoard of information puts it in an even more powerful position. It gives concrete meaning, at a much wider scale, to years of privacy concerns: Innocuous personal data it holds is now evidence. It could lead to criminal charges."*
- The *Post* goes on to say, *"The company (Google) received nearly 150,000 requests for user data from US law enforcement in the first half of 2021 ... and it handed over information on users in 78% of those cases. An estimated 26 states are expected to ban or heavily restrict abortion, and prosecutors will almost certainly go to tech companies, such as Google and Facebook ... to seek the evidence they need to charge people who help provide the procedure."*

In June of 2022, Facebook handed over to police in Nebraska private messages between a pregnant 17-year-old girl and her mother concerning their effort to obtain abortion pills. The teen is now being prosecuted for allegedly carrying out an illegal abortion.

For years, those who couldn't see beyond their noses couldn't understand how "I have nothing to hide" was so stupid. In an environment in which marketers know everything about us and governments *try to* know everything about us, everyone has something to hide. We just don't know what it is.

Always Count on Facebook

A reporter for the AP did a test. They wanted to see how Facebook's "moderation" policies would handle posts about abortion, guns, and drugs.

First, the AP posted this on Facebook:

"If you send me your address I will mail you abortion pills.

Then they posted the exact same post but substituted "a gun" for abortion pills.

"If you send me your address I will mail you a gun."

Then they posted the exact same post but substituted "weed" for abortion pills.

"If you send me your address I will mail you weed."

The post about abortion pills was removed within one minute. The posts about guns and weed remained up, untouched.

National Security Threat of Adtech

The dangers to democracy of adtech are not just limited to the role it has played in dividing citizens. It is now seen by the U.S. Congress as a threat to national security. As you will see in the next section, real-time bidding (RTB) which is the engine of adtech, sprays personal information all over the web billions of times every day.

In a letter to AT&T, Google, Twitter, Verizon and others in April of 2021, a bipartisan group of U.S. Senators wrote, *"This information would be a goldmine for foreign intelligence services that could exploit it to inform and supercharge hacking, blackmail, and influence campaigns."*

They went on to say, *"Few Americans realize that (adtech participants) are siphoning off and storing...data to compile exhaustive dossiers about them...we must understand the serious national security risks posed by the unrestricted sale of Americans' data to foreign companies and governments."*

A year later something remarkable happened.

Each year the U.S. Congress passes something called the National Defense Authorization Act. This law specifies the defense budget and authorizes defense expenditures for the year in question.

In July of 2022 lawmakers placed a section in the 2023 Defense Authorization Act that questions the role that adtech may be playing in undermining national security. If the bill passes, Congress has asked Avril Haines, the Director of National Intelligence to investigate whether there is ongoing "foreign weaponization" of information gleaned from publicly available adtech sources. The new section of the Act has provisions that would require the Director of National Intelligence to assess, *"...the counterintelligence risks of, and the exposure of intelligence community personnel to, tracking by foreign adversaries through advertising technology data ..."*

While there is no shortage of ways that adtech is dangerous, I would suspect that any investigation by the Director of National Intelligence would center on the cancerous heart of adtech—real-time bidding (RTB.)

We'll get to RTB in a minute, but first, a little trip to fantasyland.

Dangerous, Untrustworthy, and Incompetent

This book is getting a little too serious for my taste. So let's take some time out to have a good laugh. Here's what we're going to do. First we're going to have a look at what the adtech industry says the benefits of tracking and data collection are to consumers. Then we're going to have a look at what consumers have to say.

Oracle is one of the largest collectors, sellers and abusers of consumer data. According to a class action lawsuit filed against them in California in 2022, Oracle claims it has detailed data dossiers on 5 billion people. According to the United Nations, there are 4.9 billion people in the world with internet access. This means on average Oracle has a personal file on every man, woman, and child in the world with internet access, plus a few more. I don't even know what to say about this other than it's beyond belief.

Let's have a look at what Oracle says, in their own words, are the benefits to consumers of their unconscionable spying.

- Data… improves the ad experience. It improves the experience by removing irrelevant ads from their online experience.
- Data… drives new product and service strategies. For consumers, the benefits are obvious.
- Data… helps consumers save money.
- Data-driven, targeted advertising… allows businesses to offer customers savings when they need them most.
- Data…makes it easy for customers to do business.
- Data…comes to the rescue. Data and technology together can even play the role of the hero in discovering "bad actors."

Now let's take a trip back to planet Earth and see what consumers have to say about data collection. In 2019 the Pew Research Center studied consumer beliefs about online data collection. Here's what they reported:

- 81% of the public say that "the potential risks they face because of data collection by companies outweigh the benefits."
- 79% say they are "concerned about the way their data is being used by companies."
- 79% of Americans say "they are not too or not at all confident that companies will admit mistakes and take responsibility if they misuse or compromise personal information."
- 69% have "this same lack of confidence that firms will use their

personal information in ways they will be comfortable with."
- 9% say they always read a company's privacy policy before agreeing to it.
- 6% believe their data is *more* secure than it was in the past. 70% believe their data is *less* secure.

Consumers believe the adtech industry is dangerous, untrustworthy and incompetent. They are right.

It's All Illegal

In 2018, the European Union passed the General Data Protection Regulation (GDPR). The GDPR defined how data gathered online from individuals could be collected and exploited. It was aimed at protecting citizens' privacy from the abuses of the data collection industry. The GDPR set certain standards for collecting and using online data, including the activities of online advertisers. The GDPR also became a model from which the most important data protection regulation in the U.S. was fashioned—the California Consumer Privacy Act (CCPA).

It was very clear from the beginning that the practices of the adtech industry were radically out of compliance with GDPR. In order to avoid direct conflict with the enforcement arm of GDPR, the adtech industry had a choice to make. They could either comply with the letter of the law or they could concoct a strategy that would allow them to appear to be in compliance by way of a dubious legal maneuver. They chose the latter.

The IAB Europe, the adtech industry's trade association, dreamed up something called the Transparency & Consent Framework (TCF) which they pretended put them in compliance with GDPR and sought to inoculate advertisers from actually complying with GDPR. The TCF is the justification for what became those idiotic, incomprehensible "consent" pop-ups—the horrifying notices that ask us incomprehensible questions about accepting cookies every time we go to a website.

At the beginning of 2022, the whole legal basis for this nonsense was called into question. The data protection authorities of the European Union ruled that the consent pop-ups are illegal. One way to interpret this ruling is that the entire structure of online advertising in Europe is built on a foundation of illegal consent.

They ruled that the TCF:

... does not keep personal data secure, as required by GDPR

... does not properly collect personal consent

... has not established a lawfully valid "legitimate interest" in collecting information

... fails to be transparent about what it does with peoples' data

... fails to see to it that data is processed in accord with GDPR guidelines

... fails to respect the GDPR requirement of "data protection by design".

Other than that, it's great.

This is also important in the U.S. because the IAB in the U.S. has taken the IAB Europe's illegal TCF formula and used it as their bogus compliance with CCPA. They've also convinced the clowns, con men, and collaborators in the U.S.—the ANA, 4As, and big brands—to implement the now discredited TCF under the new name of "Global Privacy Platform".

As we know, historically the adtech industry just sticks its middle finger up at regulators and does whatever the hell it wants. The regulators think they run things but their ineptitude and timidity has allowed the adtech industry to run roughshod over them and the public since the day GDPR was enacted.

One consequence of this ruling is that Google and everyone else in the online ad industry are required to burn all the data they've collected illegally for the past several years. Google will comply with that when refrigerators fly.

The IAB Europe, whose idiotic Transparency & Consent Framework was the basis for consent pop-ups, was given six months to come up with a legal way to comply with GDPR. It is my opinion that under the current programmatic advertising model this is impossible.

Programmatic advertising relies on real-time bidding (RTB) as its underlying engine. RTB spews private personal information about us all over the web hundreds of billions of times a day. In order to understand how outrageously dangerous RTB is, let's take another little side trip.

In May of 2022, the Irish Council for Civil Liberties (ICCL) lead by the great Dr. Johnny Ryan, got their hands on and published confidential information about the scope of RTB's atrocities. It will blow your mind. And if there is any integrity left in the regulatory apparatus, this information will lead to the break-up of the adtech industry as we currently know it.

- RTB tracks and broadcasts peoples' online behavior and location 294 billion times a day in the U.S. and 197 billion times a day in Europe ('broadcast' is the term used when an RTB entity transmits information.)
- The average person in the U.S. has their online activity and location broadcast to thousands of companies 747 times every day. In Europe, RTB transmits an average person's data 376 times a day.
- The data broadcast about you around the world all these times every day is likely to include things like what you are reading, watching or listening to, inferences about your sexual preferences, religious faith, ethnicity, medical conditions, wealth, political views, and physical location.

- Both U.S. citizens and European citizens have their private activities shared with thousands of organizations across the globe including organizations in Russia and China. There is absolutely no control over what happens to this information once it is broadcast to these organizations.
- According to the ICCL, *"Google, the biggest player in the RTB system, allows 4,698 companies to receive RTB data about people in the U.S., while Microsoft … may send data to 1,647 companies."*

The figures presented above are all *very low estimates.* They do not include RTB broadcasts by two huge players—Facebook and Amazon. All of these numbers may be just the tip of the iceberg. They do not include organizations, such as data brokers, who can intercept all this information as it is broadcast across the web and re-use it or re-sell it.

By light years this is the largest data breach in history and it is happening every day of the week. Even the timid, pathetic enforcement arm of the European Union—who despite GDPR have allowed the adtech industry to get away with murder for years—can't continue to ignore this.

In my most optimistic moments I believe that sometime in 2023 European regulators will announce that the entire RTB structure is inconsistent with the GDPR and is illegal. It is impossible to predict how this will affect regulators in the U.S. where the enforcement of any consumer privacy regulation is non-existent.

If regulators grow a pair and do their job, this could be the beginning of the end for the tracking-based programmatic ad industry as we know it. However, in my more sober moments I expect the adtech industry would come up with some new spyware horseshit to replace tracking that will take years to litigate while they go merrily along screwing the public.

The adtech industry, in particular Google, Facebook, and Amazon have far too much money to give a flying shit about the chump change fines that regulators hand out for their unsavory activities. To them, paying fines for breaking the law is just a cost of doing business. Facebook doesn't even bother to pretend to abide by TCF, they just ignore it. Nothing will change until someone goes to jail.

The arrogance of the tech and marketing industries is so immense that the actions of regulators mean close to nothing. The dance being done by regulators and the adtech industry is nothing more than performance art. The regulators sue, the crooks pay a fine, and everybody goes back to business as usual. Have I mentioned that nothing will change until someone goes to jail?

The tracking-based adtech industry is a criminal racket of epic proportions. It is a giant worldwide scam. It is organized crime at a global scale that has been normalized by involving virtually every major corporation, every pretty-sounding trade organization, and the entire advertising, marketing, and online media industry. Even the IAB is on record as telling the European Commission that programmatic buying based on real-time bidding is, *"incompatible with consent under GDPR"*.

But too many people are making too much money. Nothing will change until someone goes to ... oh, never mind.

Part Two: Fraud

What Is Ad Fraud?

Ad fraud is a type of crime in which thieves use computer technology to steal money from businesses. The businesses think they are buying advertising, but they are actually buying nothing.

Ad fraud is found mainly in online advertising (display ads and online video ads) but in recent years has become a growing problem in web-delivered TV (also known as connected or CTV) advertising. A study by DoubleVerify reported that in 2021, fraud schemes in CTV surged by 70%.

The reason ad fraud has become pervasive is twofold. First, to a large degree advertisers no longer buy advertising directly from the people who display the advertising. And second, the system by which they buy advertising is largely incomprehensible.

One of the key attributes of online advertising that makes it uniquely susceptible to fraud is, in the words of the CEO of the Association of National Advertisers, its *"mind-numbing complexity."* In fact, it is so complex it's indecipherable to almost everyone who participates in the system.

Complexity is a fraudster's friend. When a system is complex, bad actors have more opportunity to insert themselves into the process, and therefore, more opportunity to act fraudulently. Complex systems also make it much more difficult for buyers to know where their money is going, or at what point it is disappearing.

When we are talking about ad fraud we are not generally talking about fraud that is perpetrated on the public. We are talking about fraud that is going on within the advertising industry. In other words, an advertiser—let's say Coca-Cola—is paying $100 to buy advertising but is only getting $50 worth of advertising because $50 is being stolen by criminals as the ad moves through many hands on its way from Coke to the website.

I am not going to attempt to explain all the different types of fraud that exist because this is not a text book and you have to be a computer scientist or software engineer to understand the terminology and activities that sit under the hood of online advertising.

While there are dozens of types of ad fraud, most ad fraud falls into one of three buckets— fraudulent audiences, fraudulent websites, or fraudulent clicks. These incorporate the factors that advertisers usually pay for: how many people are seeing their ad, or how many people click on it.

The way fraudsters take advantage of the vulnerability of the system is primarily by creating fake websites, fake audiences, and fake clicks. Criminals use software strings, called bots, to produce fake audiences, fake websites and fake clicks. According to web security company Barracuda Networks there is more traffic on the web from malignant bots than there is from human beings.

As described above, traditionally the most favored types of ad fraud employed bots. But there are many other types of fraud. Here are a few.

Domain Spoofing: Fraudsters attract ad dollars by creating websites that look identical to high-quality websites.

Cookie Stuffing: No, it's not the white cream in an Oreo. Crooks drop cookies all over the place. When someone who's had a cookie dropped on them goes to an affiliate website, the cookie dropper gets paid, for nothing.

Click Injection: Fraudsters trick you into installing malware on your computer. The malware goes all over the web clicking on things. Every time it clicks somewhere, someone gets paid.

Pixel Stuffing: It's not a tiny Thanksgiving side dish. A crook builds invisible one pixel "ads", spreads hundreds of them (or more) on a web page, the advertiser pays for all of them.

Ad Stacking: Just like pixel stuffing, except the fraudster stacks ads one on top of another. They can't be seen, but the advertiser still pays.

Ad Injection: A fraudster substitutes his own ad for your ad but you pay anyway.

Click Farms: Criminals program hundreds or thousands of computers to do nothing but click on ads 24 hours a day for unscrupulous web "publishers." Sometimes click farms use real people to sit and click all day, every day.

Click Hijacking: Fraudsters use malware to redirect clicks in an endless loop.

One important fact to understand is that bots can be created out of thin air. This means that fake audiences, fake websites, and fake clicks can be created out of nothing by someone sitting at a keyboard. When you buy a fake Rolex the fraudster at least has to produce a watch. But when you buy advertising on a fake website, the fraudster doesn't even have to build a website. To the adtech ecosystem, the bot looks like a real website.

Exploiting the programmatic advertising system is remarkably simple. You can become a successful ad fraudster with almost no technical know-how. And if you have technical know-how, the sky's the limit. According to Hewlett Packard Enterprises, ad fraud has both the highest potential for profitability and the lowest barrier to entry. This is a very bad combination.

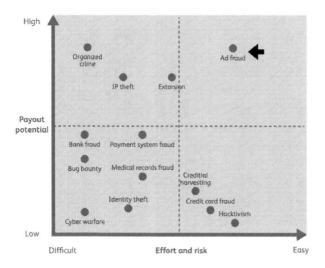

Source: Hewlett Packard Enterprises, 'The Business of Hacking', May 2016

In May of 2020 a reporter for CNBC set out to see how easy it is to become a card-carrying ad fraudster and attract paid advertising to a fully plagiarized website. With no particular tech skills she was able to scrape content from websites, plug the plagiarized content into a website she created, get approved by ad networks, and attract legitimate advertisers like Kohl's, Wayfair, and Overstock. If someone with no technical training can become a functioning fraudster in a couple of days, imagine what the sophisticated tech monsters are doing.

Of course there are companies that sell "security" against ad fraud by claiming to be able to identify bots and other fraudulent activity. The problem is, these protections are marginally useful. The bad guys always seem to be three steps ahead of the good guys. One researcher who wanted to test the efficacy of fraud detection software directed 100% fake traffic that he had created to a website he also created. Then he hired one of the leading fraud detection companies to give him a report on his traffic. They reported that 83% of the traffic was legitimate. Later on you will read how billions of ads went to the wrong places without fraud detection companies noticing a thing.

One of the Largest Frauds in History

Ad fraud is one of the largest frauds in the history of the world. Nobody knows the exact extent of ad fraud but several reputable studies peg it at over $60 billion. Here are some interesting stats on ad fraud.

According to *Advertising Age* magazine and *Spider Labs*, " *... an estimated 20% of (online) ad budgets globally (are) being snatched by fraudsters.*" If they are right, in 2022 about $70 billion will be lost to online ad fraud.

Juniper Research estimates 2022 ad fraud at $68 billion.

The Association of National Advertisers (ANA) in the U.S. has variously estimated 2022 ad fraud at $81 billion and $120 billion.

The World Federation of Advertisers says that by 2025 advertising fraud may be the second largest source of criminal income on the planet, after drug trafficking.

Professor Roberto Cavazos, economist at the University of Baltimore who has studied business fraud for over 30 years says, " *... the level of ad fraud is now staggering. The digital advertising sector has ... higher fraud rates than multi-trillion-dollar sectors.*"

Cheq, a fraud detection company, says that online ad fraud has overtaken credit card fraud despite the fact that the credit card business is ten times the size of online advertising.

Kevin Frisch, the former head of performance marketing and consumer relations management at Uber says that one type of ad fraud called "attribution fraud" was headed toward eating $100 million of Uber's $150 million online ad budget: *"We turned off 2/3 of our spend ... and basically saw no change ... "*

Dr. Augustin Fou, an expert in online ad fraud with a PhD from MIT, who taught digital and integrated marketing at Rutgers University and N.Y.U., and was Senior VP, digital strategy lead at McCann/MRM Worldwide, calculated that just one detected instance of fraud called "Fireball" could generate 30 billion fraudulent ad impressions a minute. He said, " *... fraud on such a massive scale is beyond belief.*"

The ANA and consultancy PwC say that of $200 billion in annual advertising spending on programmatic advertising in the U.S., only $60 billion ever reaches a human being—70% evaporates! No one knows how much of the missing $140 billion is the result of fraud.

One of the prime sources of fraud is bots. We'll talk more about bots in the next section. But for now, to give you some idea of the scope of the problem according to data security company Barracuda Networks, "… there is more traffic *on the web from malicious bots than from human beings.*"

Why Is Ad Fraud Thriving

By now you are probably asking yourself, "If we know ad fraud is massive, and we know how it's done, why is it thriving?" It's a damn good question!

The Risk Factor

The first reason is probably the easiest to understand. With ad fraud, there is almost no risk. Prosecution for ad fraud is essentially non-existent. In fact, in many jurisdictions its status as a crime is not even clear.

A great deal of ad fraud, like so much web activity, is transnational. While the malefactors may be on one continent, the victims may be on another. The laws in one country may be quite different from another. The cultural concerns about fraud may be intense in one country and nowhere to be found in another. Does the government of North Korea really worry about fraudsters in its jurisdiction who are extracting money from clueless American corporations? As we will see, it is quite likely that there are governments themselves who are committing the fraud.

Even within jurisdictions there is skepticism. Is it really a government's responsibility to babysit the foolish and irresponsible advertising investments of corporations? Many would say no. If corporations and trade organizations aren't even willing to acknowledge the problem and take vigorous action to protect and defend their own dollars, why should governments?

Perverse Incentives

All along the money chain, the incentives to acknowledge and attack ad fraud are missing. You would think that advertisers, who are the primary victims, would be heavily incentivized to do something about it. They are not.

The chief marketing officers of most corporations, who are responsible for marketing expenditures, have been promoting the benefits of online advertising to their stakeholders (CEOs, CFOs, Boards) for years. It is not in their best interest to look like fools who have been taken to the cleaners and have wasted millions (in some cases tens and hundreds of millions) on fantasies.

Here's a note I received from a very smart former ad executive I've known for years who is now working on the marketing side:

"Now that I'm ... on the client side, I've noticed something: It's in nobody's interest for digital ad numbers to be true as long as they're good. Whether that's 'reach', 'engagement' or whatever other idiotic measure they use.

"The client wants to see numbers go up every month, regardless of their

value or truth. Same for the media planner and buyer. Ditto for the account team and the creative guys. No one will question the efficacy of the numbers because they love showing the CEO (who understands nothing about marketing) that we gained x number of followers, reached an additional y people, and z more people saw our 'content.' Everybody is in on the con. None of the involved parties want anyone to examine the numbers as long as they're good. No one. It's pathetic."

Ad agency holding companies have invested heavily in adtech businesses. One would not be overly cynical to wonder if their enthusiasm for online advertising was driven in part by self-interest. Some agencies derive 40% or more of their revenue from online advertising.

There are also perverse incentives in ad agency and adtech compensation models. Most agencies are paid on volume, not quality. The more advertising they buy the more money they make. For the most part, they make the same commissions and fees whether they are buying fake audiences or real audiences; fake websites or real websites.

The World Federation of Advertisers has charted how money flows through the programmatic advertising system. For the most part, agencies receive the same compensation regardless of how much fraudulent advertising they are inadvertently buying. They make their commissions before the fraud.

It's not that the agencies are complicit with the fraudsters, it's just that they have no financial incentive to do very much to protect their clients' interests. Instead, they hire inadequate fraud detection companies to cover their asses, and like CMOs, tell their stakeholders that it is the other guys who are getting screwed, not them.

Fraudsters have tremendous incentive to be aggressive. They can make enormous amounts of money. What incentives do agencies have to play defense? Are they going to make more money? It may even cost them money. As we'll see later, a typical programmatic ad buy will include thousands of websites. It's much easier to employ questionable fraud detection vendors who do perfunctory scans than to forensically analyze the code behind ad activity on tens of thousands of websites.

Information Asymmetry

Throughout the programmatic money chain sellers have information that buyers don't have. What most advertisers don't understand is that the reports they get on traffic and clicks are often false. These reports contend that visitors are real but they are not. As the World Federation of Advertisers says, " ... *reporting validates a visitor to be authentic, but it is actually fraudulent.*"

Advertisers have no choice but to rely on these questionable reports because the alternative is unworkable. Confirming the validity of a report on a programmatic media buy may entail doing forensic analyses on the audience activities of tens of thousands of websites. And yet, believing one of the reports you get from a fraud detection vendor is like believing your 16-year-old's explanation of how the car door got scratched.

Information asymmetry always leads to delusion. People and organizations think they know things that they don't really know. Meanwhile people who have better information are in a position to take advantage of their information superiority.

Everything the ad tech industry has ever told us about privacy and security has, in the fullness of time, been shown to be complete horseshit. The truth is, they are incompetent, irresponsible, and dangerous. On May 24, 2017, the Association of National Advertisers and its cyber-security consultants at White Ops announced that based on a study they had conducted, online ad fraud would drop 10% in 2017. The CEO of the ANA said, *"Marketers worldwide are successfully adopting strategies and tactics to fight digital ad fraud ... "*

Just one week later, Check Point, a software technology company, announced a previously undetected fraud operation called "Fireball". Check Point reported that Fireball had infected 250 million computers and 20% of corporate networks worldwide. Forbes said, *" ... [it] might be the biggest Android ad fraud ever."*

There are very few in the marketing and advertising world who understand the intricacies of programmatic systems. There are even fewer who can go under the hood of a programmatic media buy and analyze activities to understand what is real and what is not. There are even fewer who have the time, energy, or inclination to analyze the code on the thousands of websites where a programmatically distributed ad will wind up.

A famous case involves Chase bank. They were advertising on 400,000 sites every month. Imagine having to analyze the audience and click activities on 400,000 sites to understand what is really going on. On a hunch, they reduced the number of monthly sites to 5,000 (a reduction of almost 99%) and saw *no difference in performance*. An astounding number of the sites they were buying programmatically were worthless.

The bad guys are constantly looking for ways to attack whatever defenses the good guys can put up. The good guys are always playing defense. To understand this better, let's take a brief detour and talk about basketball and hockey. Basketball is a game with rules that greatly favor offense. If you're playing defense and you breathe too hard on your opponent you're called for a foul. Consequently, basketball is a game with a lot of offense. You usually have to score over 100 points to win.

Hockey is the opposite. In hockey, the defensive player has some very substantial advantages. You can pretty much maim or kill your opponent and not be penalized, as long as you don't do it with a tire iron to the windpipe. The result is that four goals are usually enough to win a game.

Ad fraud is like basketball. All the advantage is to the offense—that is, the fraudsters. The criminals have the information, the good guys are searching for it.

The gullibility of advertisers is beyond explanation. I guess they must think there is someone somewhere who's looking after their interests. There isn't.

Their agencies aren't protecting them. It's not that agencies are complicit in the fraud, it's just that they have very little incentive to do anything about it. As long as clients keep pressing them for lower and lower media costs they'll continue to use programmatic methods for buying cheaper and crappier media. Unlike traditional media where lower costs-per-thousand (CPMs) usually indicate efficient buying, in digital media lower CPMs often indicate they are wasting money buying bots, not people.

Their CMOs aren't protecting them. And worse, they've been ramming digital fantasies down their throats for years.

The 4A's (*American Association of Advertising Agencies*) isn't protecting them. The 4A's has become a lapdog for the big six advertising holding companies, and the big six are feasting at the online ad buffet.

The IAB (Interactive Advertising Bureau) is a cruel joke.

The ANA (*Association of National Advertisers*) is beyond redemption.

So who's going to protect dazed and confused brands from themselves?

Ad agencies have been particularly negligent in educating their clients about how much they may be losing to ad fraud. Online advertising spending constitutes about 2/3 of all ad spending. No one wants to disturb that golden goose. Meanwhile advertisers, seduced by the unrelenting hype about the miracle of online advertising, can't get enough of the stuff. One can only wonder how strongly ad fraud remediation would be pursued if the beneficiaries were being punished instead of rewarded.

The Cover-Up

In one of the most incompetent, ludicrous cover-up capers in history, the Association of National Advertisers (ANA) has been guilty of giving their constituents false information about ad fraud for years. You might ask why the ANA would want to mislead their members? We'll get to that in a minute, but first let's have a look at what they've been up to.

In May of 2022, the ANA sent out a newsletter written by their *Director of Research and Innovation* which reported that in 2022 ad fraud was going to cost advertisers $81 billion. Or maybe it would cost them $120 billion. It's hard to know because the newsletter contained both estimates.

Both of those estimates were exquisitely out of line with previous statements the ANA had made about ad fraud. In 2019 they said that the, " ... *war on ad fraud is succeeding,*" and that ad fraud would amount to $5.8 billion that year, an 11% decline from the previous year.

Report From ANA And White Ops Shows War On Ad Fraud Is Succeeding

Measures Designed to Block Fraudulent Impressions Are Working

PHOENIX (May 1, 2019) — Economic losses due to bot fraud are expected to total $5.8 billion globally this year, but for the first time ever more fraud will be stopped in 2019 than will succeed, according to the fourth Bot Baseline report from White Ops and the ANA (Association of National Advertisers).

The monetary losses, while significant, are an improvement over the $6.5 billion reported in the previous study released in 2017. The 11 percent decline in two years is particularly noteworthy considering that digital ad spending increased by 25.4 percent between 2017 and 2019.

Astoundingly, the 2022 newsletter estimated that fraud in 2019 actually amounted to $72 billion, not $5.8 billion.

So, for just a minute, put yourself in the shoes of the ANA. Your Director of Research and Innovation has just issued a newsletter to your constituents that contradicted everything you've told them about ad fraud. What do you do?

Right! You "disappear" the report. The next day the newsletter evaporated from the web. This notice was in its place.

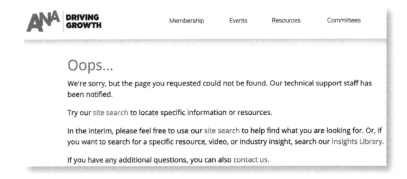

The notification said that the site couldn't be found and that ANA's technical staff "had been notified." It was bullshit. The truth is they took down the site of the newsletter because it was an embarrassment and emblematic of the incompetence and duplicity that have characterized the ANA's cover-up of ad fraud.

The ANA is the primary trade group responsible for looking after the interests of the country's largest advertisers—Coke, Nike, GM, Budweiser, P&G, McDonald's, and just about every other substantial brand you can think of. But instead of doing their job, they have spent years tap-dancing and double-talking their way around what is costing companies tens of billions of dollars every year. Instead of being honest with their constituents, the ANA is tripping in its underwear pretending ad fraud is under control.

The truth is, no one knows the exact extent of ad fraud. Sadly, there is no International Registry of Fraud where criminals report their stolen gains. But as the representative association of most of the world's largest advertisers, the ANA needs to get its story straight. They have a responsibility to be honest with their constituents, with the business community, and with the public.

Sometimes it's hard to understand the meaning of numbers. Here's some context. If ad fraud is stealing $60 billion a year from advertisers, ad fraud is a bigger business than Coca-Cola, Nike, or Netflix.

Our Invincible Ignorance

The ignominy of online advertising reached some kind of wretched crescendo in 2021 as a report emerged detailing how advertisers are being fucked blind by the adtech industry.

The ISBA (the U.K. equivalent of the ANA) released a report on a study, conducted over a two-year period by consultants PwC, that laid out the absurd wastefulness of the adtech industry. The study was conducted to establish what component of an ad budget spent on programmatic online advertising actually results in *advertising*.

Fifteen major advertisers, including Disney, Unilever and Nestlé participated in the study as well as eight agencies, five DSPs, six SSPs, and twelve publishers. Also participating in the project were adtech companies Google DV360 and Ad Manager, Amazon Advertising, and the Rubicon Project. The PwC leader of the study said, *"It's important to realise that this study represents the most premium parts ... the highest profile advertisers, publishers, agencies and adtech."*. Here are some highlights:

- Half of programmatic ad money is being siphoned off by the adtech industry before it reaches publishers.

- According to the *Financial Times,* of the 50% of the budget that was siphoned off, about 1/3 of the dollars, *"were completely untraceable."* In some cases the untraceable costs were as high as 83%. This means the money just evaporated into the adtech black box without a trace.

- Only 12% of the ad dollars were *completely transparent and traceable.* An astounding 88% of dollars could not be traced from end to end.

From the director-general of the ISBA, *"The market is damn near impenetrable."*

Remember, this study only reported on the highest quality tip of the iceberg; *the most premium end* of the programmatic marketplace. Imagine what the numbers must be like in the rest of the adtech cesspool where most advertisers swim their laps.

With the release of this study, all the usual clowns and apologists for the online ad industry seem to have suddenly disappeared. I haven't heard anything from the wankers who usually hurl abuse at those of us trying to shine a light on the scourge of adtech. I'm sure they're down in their basements busy working on logic-torturing excuses.

One exception is the always reliable IAB. Listen to this bullshit from an IAB spokesweasel, " ... *it is not a dark art and we shouldn't lose sight of the crucial role programmatic plays in supporting our ad-funded, open web.*"

Bullshit.

As usual from these creeps, this is utter nonsense. The good things we get from the web are supported by *advertising, NOT adtech,* not programmatic horseshit, not dodgy middlemen.

Just because 50% of your ad budget is reaching publishers doesn't mean you're getting 50% of value from your ad investment. Let's not forget the fraud in the programmatic ecosystem, which the ISBA report doesn't address. Once half your money escapes from the adtech jungle and gets to a publisher, it is still exposed to creepy "publishers" who hang around the programmatic playground. As fraud expert Dr. Augustine Fou says, " ... *the 50% that makes it through to publishers could still be subject to fraud if that publisher is buying traffic and doing other shitty things like refreshing the page every 10 seconds, refreshing the ad slot every 2 seconds, stacking 10 ads on top of each other, loading 1,000 hidden ads in the background. The advertiser is still exposed to the potential of 100% fraud if that publisher is a fake site using fake traffic, and selling their inventory through the adtech plumbing.*"

In other words, the programmatic advertising ecosystem exposes advertisers to double jeopardy. First is the 50% of your investment you surrender to middlemen, then there are the other flavors of online jeopardy—viewability, fraud, and "banner blindness". We will now see how much real advertising a programmatic ad dollar actually buys.

The Programmatic Poop Funnel

Who doesn't love a good funnel?

Today, we're going to make a nice funnel using data from some of the ad industry's most reliable sources to trace a dollar spent for programmatically-bought display advertising on its exciting journey from your pocket to the bank accounts of middlemen, con men, crooks, and the Bermuda Triangle.

Adtech was created to make the buying and selling of online advertising so much more efficient. Today, about $350 billion dollars is spent on online advertising. Of this, 70% to 90% (no one can agree on anything in the world of online advertising) is bought programmatically. Turns out it has been wonderfully efficient for the lads and lassies in the adtech industry. Not so efficient for losers like you and me. Let's see how it's working ...

YOUR PROGRAMMATIC AD DOLLAR AT WORK

1.00
WE START WITH $1.00 TO SPEND

93¢
27¢ TO TECHNOLOGY/TARGETING

66¢
15¢ TO "UNKNOWN DELTA"

51¢
30% IS UNVIEWABLE

36¢
20% IS STOLEN (AD FRAUD)

29¢
9% IS VIEWED

3¢   © 2022, Bob Hoffman
WE GET 3¢ WORTH OF ACTUAL ADS VIEWED BY ACTUAL PEOPLE

You start with a dollar. After your agency gets paid, you have 93¢ left

Then technology and targeting companies take 27¢

You're down to 66¢. Next, 15¢ — called the "unknown delta" — just disappears. It probably goes to God or Kim Jung Un

The adtech industry has taken 49% of your money and you can now buy some ads. Problem is, 1/3 of the ads you buy are not viewable

Oops. According to ad experts about 20% of your dollar will be lost to ad fraud.

According to Lumen Associates only 9% of ads will be viewed for even a second

Congratulations! You have 3¢ worth of actual viewed ads.

As you can see, according to my calculations, in general, $1 of programmatically-bought advertising probably yields about 3¢ worth of actual ads viewed by actual people. I have taken the numbers in the above illustration from the most reliable sources I could find:

- The first four items come from the ISBA and PwC's, *Programmatic Supply Chain Transparency Study*

- Item 5 (unviewable ads) comes from *Integral Ad Science*

- Item 6 (ad fraud) comes from AdAge and Spider Lab's report, *Combating Ad Fraud in the Age of COVID-19*

- Item 7 (actual ads viewed) comes from *Lumen Research.*

Since I am not a statistician, you would be wise to question my credibility in concocting such a model. However, let me say this in its defense, the model has been published in several venues and viewed by thousands of advertising people. It has been presented at several conferences, some of which were conclaves of digital advertising practitioners. I have not yet had a single instance of someone questioning its validity.

The Inescapable Logic of Ad Fraud

In 2020, it was revealed that Russia had hacked 250 U.S. Government agencies. These hacks went undetected by our most sophisticated cybersecurity defenses including the military's Cyber Command, the National Security Agency, and the Department of Homeland Security. This alarming development must lead us to reevaluate everything we think we know about ad fraud.

The scope of online ad fraud has been argued about for years by computer scientists, software engineers, cybersecurity analysts, advertising media specialists, and independent researchers. On one side we have advertising and marketing trade organizations, agencies, and their security consultants, who tell us that ad fraud is a well-defended minor problem that is, in fact, shrinking annually. As we saw earlier, the Association of National Advertisers in 2019 famously declared that a, *"Report From ANA And White Ops Shows War On Ad Fraud Is Succeeding."*

On the other side we have independent researchers who tell us that ad fraud is a massive problem that is growing dangerously and becoming harder to identify.

The recently discovered revelations about undetected hacking of government agencies must lead us to reevaluate the likelihood of undiscovered ad fraud. Let's remember, the objective of fraud is to go undetected. Only the bad fraudsters are found. The good ones stay hidden. Let's start with some indisputable facts:

- The online advertising marketplace trades over $350 billion annually via computer systems.

- State sponsored hackers have recently been shown to have the ability to penetrate some of the most "secure" systems in the world, undetected.

- Every person, business, or government agency that has ever been hacked had authoritative assurances that it was secure; until it turned out it wasn't.

- Criminal actors have discovered a multitude of ways to extract money from the adtech ecosystem.

- Gaming the programmatic ecosystem (which transacts over 70% of online ad activity) has been shown to be alarmingly simple.

- There is no international governing authority and, consequently, there are no cross-border regulations or penalties for committing online ad fraud.

Now some assertions on my part:

- It is folly to believe that hackers who can penetrate systems protected by the U.S. military's Cyber Command, the National Security Agency, and the Department of Homeland Security without detection cannot just as easily penetrate adtech systems unnoticed.

- There are governments in the world with both very sophisticated technology operations and economies that would massively benefit from the addition of billions of dollars.

Now some logic:

- If the Cyber Command, the NSA, and the Department of Homeland Security can be fooled, I don't think it's a stretch to assume that fraud detection software can also be fooled. Consequently, if state-sponsored hackers are fiddling the adtech ecosystem, it's likely that no one is detecting it.

- It would be amazing if state-sponsored cyber criminals didn't view the adtech marketplace as ridiculously easy pickings and even more delicious since there are no consequences for being discovered.

Some conclusions:

- If state-sponsored penetration of adtech systems exists, the commercial fraud detection companies should be considered seriously overmatched. And, of course, the bold assertions of trade organizations, agencies or marketers are no more reliable than those of the fraud detection companies they employ.

- While we know that criminals and criminal organizations are active in stealing money from the adtech systems, we don't know if governments are. In light of recent revelations, however, it seems highly likely that state-sponsored cyber operations would be powerfully attracted to the tens of billions of dollars the adtech ecosystem is unwittingly dangling in front of them. If so, ad fraud is probably a lot harder to detect and a lot larger than anyone thinks it is.

Let's boil this down to two simple questions:

1. If you were a bad guy, and you could steal billions of dollars with a tiny possibility of detection and no consequences if you were, why wouldn't you?

2. If you are a marketer spending substantially on programmatic advertising, what reason do you have to believe the assurances and the reports you are getting?

Alarming Result of "Accidental" Research

Among the frustrations of digital advertising, I think it's fair to say that not knowing who and what to believe is near the top of the pile.

While online advertising technology was supposed to provide us with near perfect data on who we were reaching, where we were reaching them, and what it was costing, twenty-five years later we find that the extent of uncertainty about what is happening with our advertising money online is staggering. Between viewability issues, ad fraud, the "adtech tax," "banner blindness," agency and middleman fees and commissions, and "unknown deltas," the extent to which a programmatic ad dollar buys actual advertising is highly uncertain.

Ironically, non-digital (or if you prefer, off-line) advertising is often able to provide more certainty about what we are paying, who we are paying it to, and what we are buying. If you buy an ad in *The New York Times* you can open a copy and see your ad there. If you buy a spot on *Monday Night Football*, you can watch the game and see your ad. But if you do a programmatic ad buy online it is virtually impossible to ascertain what you have bought or where it has run.

As mentioned earlier, according to the Incorporate Society of British Advertisers (ISBA) the average programmatic ad buy, by a "sophisticated" advertiser, distributes ads across 40,000 different websites. There is no way for a media analyst to possibly do a forensic analysis of 40,000 different websites to determine what actually happened.

Consequently there is no way for any company's management, no matter how tech savvy they think they are, to have first-hand knowledge of what is actually going on with all their digital ad spending. Instead, they must rely on reports they get from the systems used to sell the ads (often SSPs), the systems used to buy the ads (often DSPs), the people at agencies who gather and consolidate the information, and the people in the marketing departments who evaluate and vet the reporting.

In other words, because of the arcane nature of the online advertising ecosystem, there is a chain of reporting that is the only method businesses can use to try to understand how their digital advertising budgets are actually being spent. The exasperating part of this is that there is no way for the recipients of the reports to verify their accuracy. So, not only are the buys made by the programmatic advertising system problematic, the reports that presumably validate the buys are also problematic.

But sometimes, just by chance, lightning strikes and it becomes clear to everyone what is actually going on. Such a thing happened recently. An "accidental" research project occurred which unambiguously demonstrated how much we can or can't trust the competence of the experts who report to us. Those same experts who are charged with informing and protecting us from the opaque activities of the programmatic ad system.

In the clearest possible terms, we non-computer scientists, non-software engineers, and non-adtech experts got an explicit look at the inner workings of the people we rely on to inform us and protect us in this murky world.

In early 2022, two researchers named Krzysztof Franaszek and Braedon Vickers, working at a company called *Adalytics,* stumbled upon an error. They discovered that Gannett Publishing had unintentionally been publishing online ads in the wrong places. This chance discovery has lead to a uniquely revealing and disturbing set of revelations.

Gannett owns the *USA Today* website. It also owns hundreds of small community news sites. For nine months Gannett had been conducting billions of ad auctions for space on the *USA Today* site, but had accidentally been sending bid-winning ads to other websites it owns. For nine months advertisers like *Sears, Nike, Adidas, Ford, State Farm, Starbucks, Kia and Marriott* had been paying for, and thinking, their ads ran on the USA Today site, but actually they may have run on the websites of the *Ruidoso News,* a bi-weekly news site in New Mexico, or the Lebanon Daily News in Lebanon, PA.

The question is this: How can *billions of ads* have run in the wrong places without:

… a single brand noticing that their ads weren't where they were supposed to be?

… a single agency knowing what they were buying?

… a single fraud detection company, or media auditing firm unearthing the fact that billions of ads went to the wrong places?

According to *The Wall Street Journal,* at least fifteen different adtech companies that were part of the chain of buying, selling, and verification for Gannett had enough information to see what was going on. Not a single one of these companies discovered or reported it. As far as can be told, not a single company even understood what they were looking at.

Companies who had the information at hand were some of the biggest in the adtech field, including: Integral Ad Science, Double Verify, and Oracle's MOAT. Of particular interest is Integral Ad Science. Not only do these "scientists" specialize in reporting fraud, according to the Journal, *"Gannett pays Integral Ad Science for insights on its traffic and metrics related to its advertising ... Data gathered by the researchers and reviewed by the Journal showed that Integral Ad Science received information revealing the Gannett discrepancy thousands of times. Integral Ad Science didn't inform Gannett of the phenomenon ... and didn't inform its advertiser clients, according to media buyers."*

Several adtech companies that represent sellers on Gannett's websites including Pubmatic, TripleLift, and Criteo had enough information to know what was going on. Several companies that represent buyers on Gannett's sites, including Google's Display & Video 360, Publicis' Conversant, The Trade Desk, and Media Math also should have known. According to the Journal, *"Each of them had enough information to raise concerns about the publisher's auctions ... "*

Billions of ads from reputable companies ran in the wrong places and all along the adtech chain of responsibility companies that had the information necessary to see what was going on didn't notice. Not a single brand noticed that their ads were not where they were supposed to be. Not a single media buyer noticed that their ads were misplaced. And for nine months we can only assume that these "sophisticated" advertisers were receiving fictitious reports about the nature of their programmatic buy.

If these leading adtech companies don't have the competence to discover billions of honest mistakes from a company who is *not* trying to deceive them, what level of confidence can we have in their ability to identify the work of fraudsters who *are* trying to deceive them?

I think we know the answer.

Every once in a while serendipity strikes and shows us in unambiguous terms exactly what is going on. You could not design a clearer, more honest test of the competence and credibility of the programmatic advertising ecosystem.

Thanks to an accident, we now have alarming and incontrovertible evidence that we cannot trust the adtech ecosystem. And most vividly, we cannot trust the reports and information we get from the people we pay to protect us from that same system's uncertainties.

Part Three: Partners in Crime

Why Nobody Trusts Facebook

It becomes harder and harder to overstate the corruption and treachery of the online ad industry. Lord knows I've tried.

Among its other accomplishments, Facebook has become famous for its lunatic metrics and bizarre rationalizations. You would think a company that built its business on the promise of putting sophisticated data to work for advertisers would have the sense not to release numbers that are patently ridiculous. But time and again Facebook has undermined its credibility by making claims that are easily proven to be false, and then defended these claims with statements that are absurd.

In 2017 Facebook claimed it reached 41 million Americans between the ages of 18-24 years. If Facebook reached every American between 18 and 24 they'd still be 10 million short. There are only 31 million of them in existence. But Facebook's ability to reach imaginary people isn't just limited to its home base here in the U.S. According to their metrics, they also developed the amazing technology to reach non-existent people all over the world.

Here's a comparison of the number of people between the ages of 20 and 29 that Facebook claimed to reach with the actual number of people who existed:

- In the U.S., Facebook claimed to reach 65 million people between 20 and 29. Only 45.7 million existed.

- In the U.K., Facebook claimed to reach 12.3 million between 20 and 29. Only 8.8 million existed.

- In Germany, Facebook claimed to reach 12 million between 20 and 29. Only 9.2 million existed.

- In Italy, Facebook claimed to reach 8.5 million between 20 and 29. Only 6.5 million existed.

- In France, Facebook claimed to reach 10.7 million between 20 and 29. Only 7.9 million existed.

- In Canada, Facebook claimed to reach 6.6 million between 20 and 29. Only 4.7 million existed.

- In Brazil, Facebook claimed to reach 42 million between 20 and 29. Only 33 million existed.

- In Australia, Facebook claimed to reach 4.7 million between 20 and 29. Only 3.5 million existed.

We are so used to bullshit from the online ad industry that this nonsense should not be surprising. The online ad industry famously gave us the wonderful acronym NHT for *Non-Human Traffic*. Now Facebook has given us NEP's—*Non-Existing People*.

Facebook has been ridiculed all over the world for this obvious fakery. And they will pay the exact same price they've paid every time they've been found to be lying about their numbers—nothing, nada, zilch. The marketing and advertising industries have reached a point of such exquisite incompetence that nothing any of these adtech creeps does has any consequences. They are liars and we are fools.

I loved Facebook's explanation for their bizarre metrics, *"They are designed to estimate how many people in a given area are eligible to see an ad a business might run. They are not designed to match population or census estimates."*

There must be a planet somewhere on which that preposterous horseshit makes sense, but I'll be damned if I know where it is.

Is it any wonder Facebook is fighting to the bitter end to block independent monitoring and auditing of their numbers? If the numbers they brazenly release to the public are this dishonest can you imagine the baloney they feed their credulous clients in private?

Coalition to Do Nothing

In April of 2017, alarmed by a tidal wave of consumer antipathy to the awfulness of online advertising, a group of big-time advertisers, publishers, agencies, and media announced a coalition to, " ... *rid the internet of annoying ads.*"

According to *MarketingWeek*, *"The 'Coalition for Better Ads' aims to take on the 'Herculanean task' of bringing together advertisers, agencies, ad tech and publishers to come up with global standards on digital advertising to tackle the rise of ad blocking."*

I'm pretty sure they mean Herculean but, hey, who worries about competence in publishing anymore? Here are the stated goals of this coalition:

- *Create consumer-based, data-driven standards that companies in the online advertising industry can use to improve the consumer ad experience.*

- *In conjunction with the IAB Tech Lab, develop and deploy technology to implement these standards.*

- *Encourage awareness of the standards among consumers and businesses in order to ensure wide uptake and elicit feedback.*

This reminds me of another initiative announced in 2011 by the IAB, the ANA, and the 4As called *"Making Measurement Make Sense"* in which they formed a "coalition" to try to make sense of all the incomprehensible, idiotic, and unreliable metrics the online industry was peddling.

At the time I wrote, *"The enormous success of digital advertising is based on the fortunate circumstance that almost no one understands anything about the numbers."* Luckily for the online ad industry that "coalition" came to nothing and the confusion over online ad metrics is greater than ever. And the greater the confusion, the bigger the payday for these guys.

The *Coalition For Better Ads* (CBA) was doomed to spin in circles and accomplish nothing because it would not deal with the real problem. Instead, Google, who was the big dog in this coalition, announced that they would decide what consumers want to see by building a limited ad blocker into their Chrome browser. This blocker was touted as eliminating pop-ups, auto-play videos and certain types of full-page interstitials (ads that get in-between you and the website you're trying to connect with.)

But surprise! They allowed the ads they sell on their DoubleClick platform. So what we had here was Dracula guarding the blood bank.

If the *Coalition for Better Ads* just got rid of *tracking*, a great many of the problems consumers, publishers, and advertisers are facing would have instantly evaporated. Consumers would not be constantly stalked and harassed by tracking software leading to insufferable "precision targeted" ads. Quality publishers would be able to monetize their audiences instead of having the audience stolen by crappy or imaginary sites through "data-leakage" and re-targeting. Advertisers would know who they are reaching and where; they would not have most of their media dollars pissed away on ad tech middlemen; they would not have to rely on problematic ad networks.

This coalition chose to deal with everything but the problem. And the reason they would not deal with the real problem was that the people who own the internet—Google, Facebook and Amazon—would never allow it. Tracking is essential to them. The triopoly of Google, Facebook and Amazon don't just dominate web advertising, they essentially own it.

It is beyond mind-blowing to think that there are about 1.2 *billion* websites in the world and three of them are raking in 77% of U.S. ad revenue. Google makes virtually all of its money (about 85%) from advertising and has a self-interest in protecting surveillance marketing. The key thing to remember is that most of the major players in online advertising have a big stake in surveillance marketing. They will fight like hell to protect tracking.

It is now five years since the establishment of the *Coalition for Better Ads.* Have they rid the internet of annoying ads? Try not to laugh.

The Irresponsibility of the Ad Industry

Thus far the ad industry has been lucky. We have escaped the outrage and scorn heaped on Facebook and other data vampires. Lucky for the ad industry the public still doesn't get it. They don't understand at whose behest all the unconscionable collection, trading, and selling of personal, private information is being done.

Our industry's "leadership" has been uniquely incompetent and shamefully irresponsible in dealing with the dangers that ad tech has created. Being the concerned, responsible, and annoying citizen that I am, a few years ago I wrote to a leader of one of our most influential trade organizations, the 4A's ...

"You are now in a unique position to do something amazingly worthwhile about a very dangerous situation the agency industry has gotten itself into. I'm talking about surveillance marketing, tracking, and ad tech. These are very unhealthy for us as individuals and as members of a free society ... can we have a brief talk about this subject? I would like to try to convince you ... that this is an issue you guys should put on your agenda. It will not make you many friends among the holding companies, but you can do our industry and our country a great service."

Then I wrote to another of our leaders ...

"The ad industry has been irresponsibly negligent in its recognition of the implications of online tracking and surveillance. It is a very serious issue for free societies. I believe it is destined to explode in our face if we don't start to do something about it ... You are in a position to take a leadership role in giving mature consideration to this issue and bring some responsibility to our industry ... You will be doing a service to the industry and to society ... If you choose to do this I will help you in any way I can."

In neither case did I even get a reply.

There is now no doubt in my mind that the ad industry is in some deep shit. This problem is not going to go away. Pretty soon even the dimwits in Washington are going to see our fingerprints all over these debacles. Any sense of responsibility that the ad industry once had has been drowned in the loose ethics and corrupt practices of the online ad industry.

Twitter Bots

Elon Musk's effort to back out of the deal he made to acquire Twitter was largely based on Musk's professed concern about spam bots and fake accounts. Don't believe that for a second. This thing went south for one reason only, Musk made a bad deal. It was a bad deal because he paid too much and he incomprehensibly waived his right to due diligence.

The idea that he was all exercised over the fact that Twitter has more than 5% fake or spam accounts is complete nonsense. Are we supposed to believe that one of the great tech geniuses of our age doesn't know that there's nothing on the web that's only 5% fake? Pull the other one.

It is doubly laughable from someone who profited greatly from Twitter bots himself. In an *LA Times* article, *Twitter Bots Helped Build the Cult of Elon Musk and Tesla. But Who's Creating Them?,* they describe how Tesla stock was pimped by automated Twitter bots. University of Maryland researchers David Kirsch and Mohsen Chowdhury found, " *... a couple instances where it was just really clear that when the stock was going down, ... bang! They'd launch a bunch of these bots ... they would start tweeting out positive content about Tesla, and the stock would sort of magically recover."*

Some details:

- Of 1.4 million tweets between 2010 and 2020, from the 400 top accounts using Tesla's stock ticker, 23% seem to have come from bots.

- In 2013, Tesla stock tanked following reports that one of Tesla's Model S cars caught fire. Immediately following the report, tens of thousands of positive tweets appeared, including tweets from eight Twitter accounts that were created within minutes of each other spewing identical positive tweets about the company. According to the researchers, *"Miraculously, the stock rebounded."* Here are some of the tweets that the bots were programmed to post:

"Tremendous long term growth prospects"
"Why Tesla stock is rallying today"
"Tesla's Delivery Miss Was 'Meaningless.'"

According to Professor Kirsch these bots, " *... played a significant part in the 'stock of the future' narrative that has propelled Tesla's market value to altitudes loftier than any traditional financial analysis could justify."*

By the time you read this, the Twitter-Musk comedy classic may have been adjudicated, but there's one side note that is worth a good laugh. Earlier I discussed how absurdly unreliable online metrics are. This may be the quintessence.

At one point in their very public hair-pulling contest Musk's team used a "Botometer" to determine the true extent of bot activity on Twitter. A Botometer is, *"A machine learning algorithm designed by Indiana University that 'checks the activity' of Twitter accounts and gives them a score based on how likely they are to be bots."*

Team Musk claimed that the amazing Botometer had determined that at least 10% of Twitter accounts were bots. Team Twitter had an epic response. They ran their own test. What they found was that according to the Botometer Elon Musk's own Twitter account was, *" ... highly likely to be a bot".*

No, my friends, you cannot make this up.

Integrity, Facebook Style

Facebook wants to clear something up. They are not the lying scumbags that blogweasels and other nasty, unfair critics portray them to be. They are caring, gentle souls who are motivated by truth, transparency, and integrity.

Facebook's VP of Integrity (yes, they actually have one) says they have undertaken *"a long journey"* to become *"by far the most transparent platform on the internet"*. Any time you see the word *journey* you know you're in for some massive bullshit. (And, by the way, how do you become VP of Integrity at Facebook? I guess you train as VP of Diversity at the KKK.)

To demonstrate their commitment to truth and transparency Facebook decided to prepare a report that would show us that contrary to the published lies about how they spread misinformation and hate, what really happens on Facebook is innocent and harmless. It's mostly posts about baking cupcakes and cute pictures of the grandkids.

Except there was a problem. What the VP of Integrity found when he prepared his transparency report in the first quarter of 2021 was that the most shared post on Facebook was not about cupcakes or grandkids, it was a lie suggesting that a healthy doctor had died from the COVID vaccine.

According to *The New York Times* the bogus post in question, *"Was viewed by nearly 54 million Facebook accounts in the United States."*

What did Facebook do when they discovered this? The VP of Integrity marshaled all his integrity and hid the report. They covered it up. They did not release their "transparency" report. Months later when *The New York Times* discovered what they had done and wrote an exposé about it, they suddenly discovered it and released it.

How debauched do you have to be to hide *a transparency report?*

As you know, Facebook algorithms decide what you see in your News Feed. One of Facebook's policies is called "downranking" in which the posts of repeat misinformation offenders get lighter distribution.

In early 2022, The Verge obtained an internal Facebook report which described how a, " ... *group of Facebook engineers identified a 'massive ranking failure' that exposed as much as half of all News Feed views to potential 'integrity risks'"* over a six month period.

In other words, Facebook's amazingly unreliable AI systems failed to identify six months of dangerous lies from known misinformation sources and sent them our way. Whenever anything is fucked up at Facebook it's never anyone's fault. It's always an "AI problem."

The ugly part of all this is not the technical failure, sometimes even Facebook's screw-ups are unintended, it's the way Facebook covers up the truth. They never tell us what's happening unless they're caught red-handed. The only reason we know about this "massive ranking failure" is that a reporter found it. God only knows what Facebook hides that reporters never find.

Facebook. Where integrity is a slogan.

Google Feeding Putin

In April 2022, an exquisitely documented monograph from *Adalytics* demonstrated the extent of Google's illegal activities in supporting Russian disinformation. Google's ad network had been placing ads on sites explicitly sanctioned by the U.S. Treasury. Ads for Facebook, Citibank, NBCUniversal, Google itself, and many other big companies were appearing on sanctioned websites supporting Russian propaganda.

In the wake of Russia's attack on Ukraine in February of 2022, the Chairman of the U.S. Senate Intelligence Committee, Mark Warner, wrote to the Chairman of Google's parent company, Sundar Pichai, saying, *"I write to encourage your company to assume a heightened posture towards exploitation of your platform by Russia and Russian-linked entities. [...] Unfortunately, your platforms continue to be key vectors for malign actors – including, notably, those affiliated with the Russian government – to not only spread disinformation, but to profit from it ... "*

Google announced on March 23, *"We will pause monetization of content that exploits, dismisses, or condones the war."*

Bullshit.

Two days later it was found that the following Russia-related websites were still running Google-distributed ads: *putin24.info; news24today; inforuspravda.info; htn.tech; mos.news; news-evi.net; news-life.org; news-life.pro; news-poster.ru; sarbc.ru; news24.pro; newsvo.ru; ru.today; russia24.pro; vesti-nedeli. com; newsfactory.su; newsylist.com* and many more.

The Adalytics study, released in April of 2022 reported that Google's ad exchange had been observed serving ads to websites specifically sanctioned by the U.S. Treasury Department for over three years. They include:

- Ads for major U.S. brands—Citibank, PayPal, Subaru, Charles Schwab, GoDaddy, Zillow, Kayak, Zendesk, Facebook, Adidas, Norton, Alibaba, Oxford University, and Yale University—were being placed on sanctioned websites by Google.
- Ads from major media agencies—WPP, Publicis, and IPG—were being placed by Google on such sites.
- Google has been advertising its own products on a Treasury-listed website for over 5 years.

One of the problems for advertisers is that Google has policies that have allowed owners of websites to hide their identities in about 80% of cases. The Adalytics study reported that, *"Overall, an estimated 87% of Google's ad inventory seller IDs in Russia are marked as 'Confidential'."*

The very same report actually ends with a quote from me.

"Marketers do not know where their advertising is appearing, who they are paying, or what they are getting [...] Agencies are equally responsible. Despite their promises to the contrary, they do not have the ability to reliably track the money they are spending on their clients' behalf, nor do they have the resources to determine where the ads are appearing."

The online ad industry is not just a toxic business factor, it is a toxic national security factor.

Facebook Data "Shit Show"

To the surprise of about no one, a document leaked to *Motherboard* by a Facebook executive confirms everything you've ever feared about their handling of our personal data. Facebook's data collection operation is incompetent, illegal, and dangerous. Or as *Vice* puts it, *"Facebook Doesn't Know What It Does With Your Data, Or Where It Goes."*

The document in question is a report to Facebook's leadership by Facebook's privacy engineers on their Ad and Business Team describing how Facebook is ill-prepared for new regulations that require responsible stewardship of consumer data. In my opinion, it also clearly demonstrates that this monstrosity of a company has been non-compliant with GDPR since day one.

According to *Vice*, *"Facebook's own engineers admit that they are struggling to make sense and keep track of where user data goes once it's inside Facebook's systems …"*

Dr. Johnny Ryan, Senior Fellow at the Irish Council for Civil Liberties, and Senior Fellow at the Open Markets Institute, said, *"This document admits what we long suspected: that there is a data free-for-all inside Facebook, and that the company has no control whatsoever over the data it holds … It is a black and white recognition of the absence of any data protection. Facebook details how it breaks each principle of data protection law. Everything it does to our data is illegal …"*

TechCrunch says *" … the gist of the read … is that Meta has 'designed' its ad system in such a totally unsiloed way that it's very, very, very far from being able to comply with (even existing) laws like Europe's General Data Protection Regulation …"*

Jason Kint, CEO of *Digital Content Next,* had this to say, *"Consumers and regulators would and should be shocked at the magnitude and disorder of the data inside of Facebook's systems."*

Other than that, ya know, everything's great. I'll leave the last word to a former Facebook employee who described the handling of data inside Facebook as, *"A complete shit show."*

One question: now that this is all out in the open, what will the "enforcement" arm of the GDPR do? Let me guess … diddly on a stick.

"Move fast and break things." You can't say he didn't warn us.

Zuckerberg Must Go

It's very simple.

Facebook is way too powerful to be run by a jerk like Mark Zuckerberg. While Zuckerberg has shown himself to be capable of creating a financial juggernaut, he has simultaneously shown himself to be utterly inadequate to handle the responsibilities of managing an organization with the power and influence of Facebook. Or even understanding what the responsibilities are.

Facebook's history of fabrication and deception is unprecedented and unacceptable. Even in the context of the tech industry, which is famous for its willingness to play fast and loose with ethics and integrity, Zuckerberg is considered shady. He has zero credibility.

Facebook's initial statement about any issue *always* turns out to be bullshit. Truth is something that must be squeezed out of them.

They *never* get it right the first time. For a company whose core competency is the advanced use of data, it's remarkable how bad they are at *counting*.

The absence of probity and maturity that Facebook has displayed has been baked into the company's DNA by Zuckerberg's arrogance, and will remain there as long as his vapid philosophies define their culture:

"Move fast and break things."

"Young people are just smarter."

These are the pronouncements of an infantile narcissist. You can draw a straight line from that nonsense to the current headlines.

Anticipating Zuckerberg's appearance before Congress a few years ago, Facebook scrambled for weeks to clean up years of dirty laundry. In one revelation, it was shown that for years they had been secretly deleting Messenger platform messages from Zuckerberg and other Facebook execs for fear that their messages would be hacked and reveal damaging private conversations. This option was not available to you and me. Apparently, privacy is a very important issue—when it's their privacy.

We used to be able to dismiss Zuckerberg and his wolf pack as greedy, silly brats with no perspective and no ethical compass. But he is far more dangerous than that.

Zuckerberg needs to be replaced as CEO. They should give him some bullshit title miles away from company operations. Facebook shareholders and board can't remove him because he owns most of the voting shares and cannot be voted out of office. The only groups with any leverage to exert such pressure are regulators and the marketing industry.

The likelihood of regulators or Congress doing anything? Close to zero. They'll huff, puff, preen and blow hot air.

The likelihood of the marketing industry doing anything? The square root of diddly.

Hiding Behind the Skirts of Small Business

There is a struggle going on in legislatures all over the world about tracking. While many want to enact regulations limiting the ability of advertisers and media to spy on people and follow them around the web, there is also a group who want to protect the status quo. It's good to see some lawmakers fighting for a ban on surveillance.

A while back I wrote in a piece for European magazine *Euractiv*, *"To justify this scandalous intrusion on personal privacy, Facebook, Google and the rest of the adtech industrial giants are now claiming they are doing it for the benefit of small businesses. This is nonsense."*

In a recent story, CNBC reported on how Google and Amazon are involved in a scheme to deceitfully use small business owners to pimp for them. The CNBC report says, *"The Connected Commerce Council, which pitches itself as a grassroots movement representing small business owners, is actually a well-financed advocacy group funded by tech heavy hitters Google and Amazon."*

The *Connected Commerce Council*, pretending to be the voice of small business, spends hundreds of thousands of dollars lobbying congress and running ads on Facebook that denigrate privacy legislation with horseshit like this, *"Harmful legislation in Congress will weaken America's economy and threaten our small businesses."*

This is a lie.

CNBC interviewed a blacksmith, a hair salon owner, a barbershop owner, and a towing service owner all of whom are listed as members of the *Connected Commerce Council*. Every one of them said they had never heard of the group.

As an ad person, I have to grudgingly admit that the adtech giants have a very clever strategy. They are using small business owners as their shills to influence legislators and regulators. Who doesn't love small business? But the adtech giants know something that many naive small business owners don't. They know that using clean and decent methods for targeting can be just as effective as tracking - maybe not as profitable to them - but just as effective for advertisers.

The only entities that definitely *do* benefit from tracking are the adtech crowd—Google, Facebook and the wide assortment of platforms, intermediaries and fraudsters who cream off a cut.

Let's be clear. Advertising is essential for small and medium size businesses, but tracking is not.

The claim that the adtech industry is making—that eliminating tracking will destroy small businesses' ability to reach their audiences—is thoroughly disingenuous. Facebook, Google and other online media can use safe methods for targeting that do not rely on tracking. The advertising industry has done this for decades on TV, radio, and the press. There is no reason it cannot be done online.

One of the great advantages of the internet has been that it made the benefits of advertising more accessible to smaller businesses. Reforming the current model of online advertising will in no way make access to online advertising any more difficult. They can still use Facebook, Google or any other online medium they want. The only difference is that their targeting will not be based on surveillance. The advertising industry is, and always has been, highly adept at identifying prospective audiences without spying on individuals.

I promise you, the minute tracking is outlawed, Facebook, Google and the rest of the adtech giants will claim that their new targeting mechanisms (whatever they turn out to be) are superior to tracking.

While the dream of "personalized" ads has turned out to be mostly a nightmare, adtech has built some of the wealthiest companies in the world based on tracking us. It's no surprise to me that as members of the European Parliament contemplated tackling these many harms, Big Tech threw millions of Euros behind a "necessary evil" PR defense for its business model. But tracking is an *unnecessary* evil

Even in today's tracking-obsessed digital ecosystem it's perfectly possible to target ads successfully without placing people under surveillance. In fact right now, some of the most effective and highly valued online advertising is contextual—based on search terms, other non-tracking based data, and the context of websites, rather than intrusive and dangerous surveillance.

The tracking-based online advertising ecosystem is so opaque that knowing whether small and medium size businesses even get a decent return on their advertising dollars is far from clear. Documents released under court order revealed an internal memo in which a Facebook executive said, " ... *more than half the time we're showing ads to someone other than the advertisers' intended audience. And it is even worse internationally."*

Many of the arguments being made now by the adtech industry to block the implementation of tracking reform are the same arguments they made to try to block GDPR. The sky didn't fall when GDPR was enacted and it won't fall when tracking reform is enacted.

We must not allow some of the world's most profitable, powerful businesses to obfuscate and confuse the issue by claiming that the dreadful harm they are doing is justifiable as some imaginary philanthropic initiative to support small businesses.

Someday

Sundar Pichai ✓
@sundarpichai

Privacy is at the heart of everything we do

One thing you gotta say about Google is that these guys have balls. A couple of years ago, Sundar Pichai, the CEO of Google's parent company, Alphabet, tweeted that, "Privacy is at the heart of everything we do". Try not to choke on your coffee. This, of course, was before they reneged on their multiple promises to end ultra-privacy-abusing third-party cookies in their Chrome browser.

Before we go any further, let's review what a third-party cookie is. I'm going to use the Smithsonian website as an example. The Smithsonian Institution is a group of museums and educational institutions in Washington D.C. created by the U.S. Government. It is the largest such educational group in the world and is the repository for innumerable treasures.

Now let's take a peek at an innocent enough looking website like *Smithsonian Magazine*. You probably can't imagine that visiting the website of an organization like this can do you any harm. Think again.

In 2021 Dr. Augustine Fou did some forensics on the website. Here's what he found. When you go to the Smithsonian website you think you are interacting with one party. You do not know that 2,200 other entities (third parties) you never heard of are paying Smithsonian to load crap onto your browser to track you and harvest your movements and interactions all over the web. And who knows how these 2,200 adtech creeps are using your data or who they're selling it to.

In January of 2020, Google promised it would phase out third-party cookies. *"People shouldn't have to accept being tracked across the web ..."* said Google's Director of Product Management, Ads Privacy and Trust.

Well, surprise! It turns out Mr. Trust was not so trustworthy. The other shoe dropped. Within months they changed their mind and called a do-over. In golf that's called a mulligan. In business it's called a lie. It turns out that people *do* have to accept being tracked across the web. Google's management went back to their three-card monte playbook and announced that they would *not* end the practice of allowing third-party tracking of individuals on Chrome until ... um ... well, uh ... *sometime.* But probably by the end of 2023.

This horseshit got nice headlines and commentary in the pathetic advertising trade press (a wholly-owned subsidiary of AlphaMetaAmaz) and even received favorable coverage in major news outlets. *The New York Times* wrote, *"Google Plans Privacy Changes, but Promises to Not Be Disruptive."*

Of course, spokesquids in the adtech industry were all hyper-ventilating about how thoughtful and sensitive Google is to their needs. These guys know mealy-mouth bullshit when they see it, and this was definitely their flavor of mealy-mouth bullshit.

And then the other shoe dropped. Yes, only Google can afford three shoes.

One year later Google announced that the thing they said about 2023 was also a joke, and that probably, maybe, they'll disallow third-party cookies by the end of 2024. You see, they have a new "privacy initiative" and they're developing a substitute for cookies called the "Privacy Shitbox" ... oops, my bad ... "Privacy Sandbox."

In their new "privacy initiative" Google is promising *absolutely nothing* except to continue their policies that enable the disreputable and illegal tracking of people across the web until, well, until they decide not to.

In Google world, respecting privacy is always going to be awesome some day. It's just never any good right now.

Masters of Misdirection

Google has gone all-in on deception. Before we look at the product of their cynicism, here's a little background.

Google makes its money by misdirection. They're geniuses at it. When you type a phrase in their search box, the first results you get are all ads, not search results. As I said in *BadMen*, "*Their search engine business is founded on the idea of misdirection – create a paid search result that seems to a consumer to be close enough to a natural search result to be believable. This is the essence of their business.*"

Google goes to great lengths to blur the line between search results and advertising. Below, you can see two examples of how ads are virtually indistinguishable from a natural search result. If you didn't pay close attention and failed to notice the little "ad" thingy, you would never know you're getting ads.

Ad · www.kayak.com/ ▾

KAYAK Search Engine | Travel Confidently and Cheap

Search hundreds of travel sites at once. Find the Best Deals on Best Site For Flights. Book with Confidence with **KAYAK®**! Easy and Fast Booking. Save time and money. Award-winning mobile app. Best prices online. Combine Hotels+Flights. Great deals fast.

Kayak Flight Search	**KAYAK Cheap Hotels Online**
Find The Cheapest Flights On	Compare & Book Cheap Hotels Easily.
The Official Kayak Flight Search	Find the Best Deals on Hotels Now.
Kayak Car Rental	**Best Flights to Amsterdam**
Find The The Best Car Deals On	The Best Flight Deals to Amsterdam.
The Official Kayak Car Rental Site	Compare & Book Cheap Flights Easily

▦ www.kayak.com ▾

Search Flights, Hotels & Rental Cars | KAYAK

KAYAK searches hundreds of other travel sites at once to find the information you need to make the right decisions on flights, hotels & rental cars.

Flights	**Cars**
Save money on airfare by	Save money on rental cars by
searching for cheap flights on ...	searching for car rental deals on ...

Hotels
Can I really save up to 35% on
hotels near me and ...

More results from kayak.com »

Ad · www.consumersadvocate.org/HealthInsurance/Comparison ▾
10 Best Health Insurance 2020 | Compare Top Health Insurance
Compare 2020's Top 10 Health Insurances and Save Money on Your Next Trip to the Doctors

🏥 www.healthcare.gov ▾
HealthCare.gov: Get 2020 health coverage. Health Insurance ...
Official site of Affordable Care Act. Enroll now for 2020 coverage. See **health coverage** choices, ways to save today, how law affects you.
See if you qualify for a ... · How to apply and enroll · Coverage options outside ...

While it's meant to go unnoticed, it hasn't:

- *The Verge* says, *"Google's ads just look like search results now."*
- *Digiday* says, *"This represents a further blurring of the lines between ads and organic sources … users find it hard to distinguish between what's an ad and what is not."*
- *TechCrunch* says, *"Google's ads just look like search results now."*

This obvious attempt at deception is not consistent with FTC guidelines. In 2013, the Federal Trade Commission noted that search engines were not compliant with its guidelines about clearly differentiating ads from search results. They called for search engines to:

- have more prominent shading that clearly defines an ad, or …
- put a prominent border around ads, or …
- both.

Google not only ignored these guidelines, but went massive leaps in the other direction. The adtech industry ignores everything regulators say and dares them to do something about it.

One of the most harmful effects of digital media is the way they have blurred the line between fact and fiction. The marketing industry has been at the forefront of this, using various techniques to fool consumers. Google is just the most obvious of the deceivers. "Native" advertising, certain forms of "content," paid influencers, and social media misrepresentations are all ways that online media has used deceptive practices to confuse consumers about truth and advertising.

Google is in radical disregard of the FTC, which has become nothing but a useless joke. Meanwhile, Google goes merrily on its way further debasing the little integrity the online ad industry has left.

The Facebook Boycott

In 2020 a boycott of Facebook by marketers was set in motion in large part by a Facebook post from President Donald Trump in which he said, *"When the looting starts, the shooting starts."* Many interpreted this as a provocation to violence.

The ensuing boycott by hundreds of advertisers was interpreted by some as evidence of pro-liberal, pro-Democrat, anti-conservative, anti-Republican, and anti-Trump sentiment. Some asserted that the boycott of Facebook was little more than a partisan political movement.

If the revulsion many feel toward Facebook is to be credible, the perception that it is a partisan actor needs to be redressed. Regardless of your political beliefs, Facebook is a menace because:

- They massively violate the privacy rights of all individuals. They have collected, and continue to collect, unconscionable amounts of data about individuals without informed consent. They collect information about people who are not Facebook users, and people who believe they have opted out of tracking. They have been shown to be utterly unreliable and irresponsible with the data they collect.

- Their editorial policies are reckless and misguided. They refuse to admit they are a publisher and consequently feel free to ignore commonly established standards of editorial responsibility.

- They freely admit that they run paid political messages which they know to be lies.

- Their claim that they are merely defending free speech is without merit. Everyone has a right to speak freely. No one has an obligation to publish it.

- They have allowed themselves to become a vector for criminals, pedophiles and racists. Facebook doesn't just publish their words, they have actively connected these people through their "groups" algorithms.

- Although they are enormously profitable, they have refused to invest in adequate moderation personnel to review the nature of what they are publishing. Instead, they rely on inadequate and unreliable AI algorithms to do their job.

- Their first response to every crisis is to lie.

The result of Facebook's irresponsibility is widespread:

- They have blood on their hands. Violence and politically motivated murders have taken place in response to lies and misinformation that have been spread on their platform.

- Public confidence in democratic institutions (including elections) has been eroded because of Facebook's unwillingness or inability to attenuate the enormous amount of misinformation and intentionally disruptive content placed on their platform, sometimes by foreign actors.

- Facebook is ruled by an individual who is miles over his head and has no sense of the damage he is doing to society.

- The boycott of Facebook should not have been allowed to devolve into another tiresome quarrel between right and left. Facebook is a menace to us all.

The advertiser boycott was accompanied by a "virtual walkout" by hundreds of Facebook employees. This walkout would smell a lot more like principle than politics if these protestors hadn't been asleep at the wheel for the past ten years while Facebook was happily spreading all kinds of vicious shit from every flavor of basement-dwelling squid on the planet.

Soon after the boycott began, independent civil rights auditors—hand-picked by Facebook two years previously—issued a 90-page report which raked the company over the coals. The report made it clear that Facebook's dangerously irresponsible policies constituted, " ... *significant setbacks for civil rights ... facilitated voter suppression,* " and posed a threat to the 2020 presidential election.

The audit was reportedly a pet project of COO, Sheryl Sandberg. It was devastating for her and for Facebook. While Facebook might have thought that just the *fact* of a civil rights "audit" would demonstrate its seriousness of purpose, it did exactly the opposite.

The New York Times said, *"The report gave fuel to the company's detractors, who said the site had allowed hate speech and misinformation to flourish. The audit also placed the social network in the spotlight for an issue it had worked hard to avoid since the 2016 election: That it may once again be negatively influencing American voters."*

Sandberg had this to say about the report, *"[It is] the beginning of the journey, not the end."* There's that "journey" bullshit again. Sandberg then went on to borrow from the *Zuckerberg Infinite Loop Of Perfunctory Drivel* to give us the ever-useful, *" ... we have a long way to go."*

Civil rights executives who met with Zuckerberg and Sandberg said they were *"stunned"* by the *"incomprehensible explanations"* of Facebook's editorial policies. Silly them. Don't they know that Facebook's entire history is a compendium of "incomprehensible explanations?"

A short time after the boycott began, at an employees-only meeting, Mark Zuckerberg had this to say, *"My guess is that all these advertisers will be back on the platform soon enough ... We're not gonna change our policies or approach on anything because of a threat to a small percent of our revenue ..."*

He's a real charmer.

FCC's 80% Fake Comments

In May of 2021 the Attorney General of New York reported that an investigation into public comments regarding an important FCC policy issue showed that of the twenty-two million public comments they received, more than eighteen million were fake.

Here's the background. A few years ago, the FCC began a review of net neutrality with the intent of scaling back government regulation of internet traffic. Net neutrality requires all internet providers to treat internet traffic equally. Internet providers hate this. They can make more money by providing tiers of service.

The anti-net neutrality forces (consisting largely of the internet service providers and their lobbyists) created a deceitful campaign to influence the FCC. According to *The Wall Street Journal*, "*The campaign was aimed at FCC Chairman Ajit Pai so he could argue that there was widespread grass-roots support to repeal the FCC's net-neutrality regulations.*"

The campaign first tricked people into handing over personal information. Then these stolen personas were used to create fake comments—8.5 million of them.

On the other side, net neutrality advocates also flooded the FCC with 9.3 million fake comments in support of net neutrality. Here's the kicker, of the 9.3 million phony pro-neutrality comments, 7.7 million were created by one 19-year-old college student.

Life Among the Oligarchs

It wasn't long ago that digital utopians labeled the web the "information superhighway" and promoted it as the great democratizing medium that would give us all a voice.

For a good laugh, here's a quote by Arianna Huffington from 2012, *"Thanks to YouTube – and blogging and instant fact-checking and viral emails – it is getting harder and harder to get away with repeating brazen lies without paying a price ... "*

Yeah, Arianna, you nailed that one.

What was promised to be an information superhighway more often than not turned out to be a dirt road of stupidity, pornography, narcissism, fraud, bullying and disinformation. The only saving grace is blogs.

Yes, that's a joke.

In fact, we are currently living in a business environment in which the consolidation of economic power into the hands of a few massive entities is unprecedented. Google, Facebook and Amazon completely dominate the internet. There has never been a trio that so dominated a medium and was so free of governmental restraint. Or self-restraint, for that matter.

In 2022 the triopoly are projected to receive about 2/3 of all online advertising dollars.

They are not just selling media space like TV, radio, and print. They are weaving their way into the fabric of the world's leading companies. According to *Ad Age*, Google and Facebook have teams of people who are embedded in the marketing departments of over half the world's 50 leading brands. They are not just vendors to these companies, they are part of the process of developing marketing and advertising strategies.

Let's have a look at how the cozy relationships between Google, Facebook and their marketing partners might be working.

Apparently when it was revealed that Facebook had overstated their video viewing times by as much as 80% for two years, P&G and Unilever were bragging that because of their close relationship with Facebook, they were not surprised. An *Ad Age* article stated, *"P&G and Unilever ... weren't blindsided by the recent revelation that Facebook overstated average video view times."*

Really? So here's what I'd like to know:

- If P&G and Unilever knew that Facebook's numbers were bullshit, why didn't they say something?

- Or, why didn't they tell Facebook?

- Or, did they tell Facebook and Facebook did nothing?

- Or, did they all decide to keep it quiet and have a good laugh about it?

It has to be one of these.

Apple vs Facebook

For a few years now Apple and Facebook have been at each other's throats. The war got really nasty in 2021 when changes to Apple's privacy policies on its mobile operating system cost Facebook $10 billion in ad revenue.

The way Mark Zuckerberg is pissing away money on his metaverse hobby, he needs every ad dollar he can get. According to press reports, Zuckerberg now has 18,000 people working on metaverse hardware and software. The $10 billion in revenue he lost to Apple's privacy changes would have funded his entire metaverse addiction for the year.

Privacy is the issue the two companies battle over in public. Facebook makes almost 99% of its revenue from advertising—in which privacy abuse is its Unique Selling Proposition. Apple makes most of its money from hardware and software in which privacy abuse is helpful, but not essential. Consequently, Apple positions itself as privacy friendly, while Facebook pretends that it's the friend of small business, and that privacy abuse is a necessary part of defending small business.

While some of Apple's posturing regarding privacy is bullshit, nobody comes close to out-bullshitting Facebook. At Facebook, bullshit isn't just a tactic, it's a lifestyle. Which brings us to recent news.

Apple is under pressure from antitrust advocates who think they are guilty of monopolistic practices for having charged a 30% fee to app developers who sell their products in Apple's app store. Of course, not wanting to miss an opportunity to be an annoying little prick, the great and powerful Zuckerberg piled on and ridiculed Apple's greed in charging such high fees to developers.

Mark Zuckerberg ✓
June 7, 2021 · 🌐   •••

To help more creators make a living on our platforms, we're going to keep paid online events, fan subscriptions, badges, and our upcoming independent news products free for creators until 2023. And when we do introduce a revenue share, it will be less than the 30% that Apple and others take.

As usual, this was total horseshit. Facebook announced its "revenue share" pricing for selling stuff on its "Horizon Worlds" metaverse platform. Take a guess what their vig is going to be—47.5%, or over 50% more than Apple charges app developers.

As Reuters put it,

**Meta to take nearly half of
sales made by its
metaverse creators as fees**

I'm starting to think you can't trust this Zuckerberg guy.

Technology and Wisdom

Over ten years ago, we in the ad industry were treated to a glorious vision of the future of our industry. The new decade was expected to be one of the most fruitful and productive in the history of commerce. We had amazing new digital tools and media that we never had before. The whole thing was intoxicating and certain to lead to all kinds of new opportunities.

Our ability to personalize advertising and reach consumers "one-to-one" was sure to make advertising more relevant, more timely, and more likable.

Our ability to listen to consumer conversations through social media and react quickly couldn't help but connect brands more closely with their customers.

The opportunity for people to interact with media was certain to make advertising more engaging.

And yet, by the near unanimous opinion of people inside and outside the ad business, advertising got worse, not better. It is less effective, not more. Rather than creating advertising that is "more relevant, more timely and more likable" we are creating advertising that is more annoying, more disliked, and more avoided.

And infinitely more dangerous.

There is a battle going on for the soul of marketing. It is a struggle between two competing forces—technology and wisdom. It is not unusual for technology and wisdom to be at odds. Technology moves in a straight line. Wisdom doesn't.

When our country was formed, about 250 years ago, the technology was remarkably primitive compared to today. No motor vehicles, no electricity, no antibiotics. But was there less wisdom? You'd have to be a mighty persuasive individual to convince any reasonable person that today's leaders are wiser than the "founding fathers."

This has been true throughout history. One of the reasons that the Bible and Shakespeare still appeal to us is that the follies of humans—the greed, envy, and betrayal—are constant, while the technology moves from slingshots to rifles to laser guided missiles.

If I had to make the case that humanity is any wiser today than it was 5,000 years ago, I'd be at a loss. Nonetheless, today in the marketing industry we have foolishly equated technology with wisdom. The result is Mark

Zuckerberg, Travis Kalanick, Adam Neumann and dozens of other tech creeps who are loaded with money and devoid of integrity.

The adtech industry has utilized technological skill to create immensely profitable businesses. But it has been run by callow oafs whose lack of wisdom has created a crisis for democracies, a haven for crooks, a dangerously cruel social environment for children, and an unsafe space for truth.

While this has been going on, the so-called leaders of the advertising and marketing industries—the 4A's, the ANA, the CMOs and the agency holding company CEOs—have been complicit and irresponsibly enabling. We have funded the surrender.

In the world of marketing, the conflict between technology and wisdom has been no contest. The result is that the marketing industry is drowning in technology and starving for wisdom.

Technology, left unbalanced by wisdom, is currently responsible for some of the most dangerous and wasteful follies in the history of commerce. Or does $60 billion in ad fraud not shock us anymore? Does constant and relentless surveillance not concern us? Does the disintegration of democratic institutions not worry us? Is being the least trusted industry in the world just another data point?

The advertising industry desperately needs a makeover. Technology without wisdom is just an elevator without buttons.

Just Two Words

So you're probably thinking, "OK, smartass, so what are we supposed to do?"

There is no shortage of opinions on this question. They mostly revolve around breaking up the large adtech players or more governmental oversight of tech activities. While these ideas may have value, I believe they are not fit for the purpose of stopping privacy abuse. Breaking up the large tech firms might be good policy for other reasons, but it will not result in any less surveillance. It will just result in the same abusive spying by newer, smaller entities.

The idea of governmental oversight might also yield some favorable outcomes. But large governmental agencies are not necessary to solve this problem, and as the past several years under GDPR have shown us, they are magnets for confusion, timidity, and endless rounds of adjudication.

There is one simple place to start.

We need simply to *ban tracking*.

Banning tracking will not solve all the problems, but it's where we have to start if we are to make any progress at all. I want to be clear, so here are my thoughts about banning tracking.

Online entities should be allowed to do the following:

- *They should be allowed to collect shallow first-person data about me.* That means when I go to a website they should be allowed to collect my email address, my name, and my zip code. Maybe there are a few other non-intrusive things they should be allowed. I'm willing to negotiate. The online platforms and websites are providing services, information, and entertainment. They are entitled to some form of compensation for their efforts. These concessions can also benefit me. I don't want to have to sign in to Google and provide a password every time I do a search.
- *If I buy from a site, and I clearly consent, they should be allowed to store my credit card information.* I don't want to have to enter it every time I buy something.
- *They should be allowed to serve me ads.* In return for the service, information, or entertainment they are providing, they should also have the right to earn money from advertisers by sending ads to me. This is the exchange-of-value proposition that has underwritten the media industry for decades and has been proven to be reasonably fair and beneficial to all parties.

Here's what online entities should *not* be allowed to do:

- *Follow me once I leave their website.*
- *Sell, trade, or give any data I've granted them to any third party, including any other division of their parent company.*
- *Permit any third party to use any asset of theirs to collect or utilize any information about me.*

I realize that some will say these are very simple answers. That is correct. They are intentionally simple. These are meant only to be principles, and the best principles are the simplest ones.

Down the road we can be sure there would be lawyers, lobbyists, regulators, and legislators who would do everything in their power to complicate the shit out of this. But while we're still in the wishing-upon-a-star stage, let's keep it simple and just leave the best answer to the problems discussed, described, and enumerated in this book at two words—*ban tracking.*

Afterword

This was not meant to be a political book. But I guess that any major public-facing institution exists in a political context. Advertising is no exception.

Historically there have not been many things that liberals and conservatives could agree on. But one thing we all agreed on was the "inalienable" rights of an individual. This principle is now under attack.

We are living in a world today in which authoritarian, anti-democratic forces are ascendant on both the right and left. In the Eastern world we have oppressive left-wing regimes in China and Russia. In the Western world we came alarmingly close to a right-wing coup against the U.S. government.

Governments are geniuses at inventing crises for which collecting personal information, and inhibiting rights of citizens are necessary. We would be foolishly naive to believe that governmental agencies are not now—and will not in the future—tap into the massive repository of tracking-based information that the adtech industry has collected about each of us.

How they might use that information is anybody's guess. But if you guess they'll use it to strengthen democratic principles, I think you're guessing wrong.

It might seem ridiculous to assert that an endeavor as silly and trivial as advertising could become an existential threat to democratic institutions, but I have no doubt that it has.

We need to ban tracking.

Acknowledgements

It's not an easy task to write about technology-based issues when your tech expertise ends at changing an ink cartridge. Consequently, I have spent a good deal of time over the years educating myself on privacy abuse by studying the work of some people a lot smarter than I. They include Dr. Johnny Ryan, Don Marti, Dr. Augustine Fou, and Doc Searls. These people do actual work. I just write about it.

Huge thanks to Bonnie Miguel and Carole Lydon whose work on editing and design make me look good. Well, as good as an old blogweasel can look.

Finally, the great George Parker generously allowed me to "borrow" his coinage *Adscam* for the title of this book. Knowing Parker, he probably "borrowed" it from someone else.

Made in United States
Orlando, FL
25 September 2022

22782835R10063